The   PoPedology
of an
Ambient   Language

Edwin   Torres

a t e l o s

29

Grateful acknowledgement is made to the editors of the following publications in which some of these poems first appeared: *The Best American Poetry 2004, The Brooklyn Rail, Explosive, Heights Of The Marvelous, Kenning, Longshot, Lungfull, and Split 180.*

The core of the last section, *The PoPedology of an Ambient Language*, was based on a *Poetry & Pedagogy* symposium at Bard College, transposed into a lecture for Naropa University, adapted as a radio play for WPS1.org and now appears in these pages in its final incarnation. This book was produced while in residence with Lower Manhattan Cultural Council.

The author wishes to thank Lyn Hejinian and the vision of Atelos Books for the invaluable opportunity to stretch out, Elizabeth & Rubio Jett, Marjorie Welish for her sage advice, the resident LMCC artists at 120 Broadway for their inspiration through the hallways, and all drifters, nomads, seers, seekers and creatures who live in their language.

Ŧ Atelos

A Project of Hip's Road
Editors: Lyn Hejinian & Travis Ortiz
Cover & Book Design: Edwin Torres

for Rubio

ELECTROBABBLEIST

WALLISM

I
II
III
IV

THE POPEDOLOGY OF AN AMBIENT LANGUAGE

The PoPedology of an Ambient Language

ELECTROBABBLETST

QUARK TRICK

decorative heart slap
chasing zephyr tail

wearing red for aerial diffusion
elusive illusion reached by ruin

how to render gesture
before its mess: preferection

how to gale on DNA
while still revered by extension

the whirligigged dog arrives
bowlegged in blue surrender

how to pierce insistent whelping
tracking helium protector

bowing calendrical wow
over cumulus encryption

how to mensa the masses
before caffeinating pavarotti

how to aria the rooftops
running wicked over nympho

how to lend a hand
chasing tail with a shut mouth

AND SOME CAME RUNNING

world is lover
questioning lack of understandment
i am lover
unconditioned for rejectals

fractals of acceptance
are skin pores of world
where i place unforged energy unconditional
into world

like lover roaming bodyscape
with unbridled tongue
world has need
to understand me

i don't understand world
but still i love her
want world to not understand me back
to love me for just showing up

lazy?   fate?   precarious preoccupation with visceral languing?
maybe

language is tongue
to sense hidden crevice
to discover fractured cablings
waiting for instruction

i am lover   in position for climax
world   too interested in foreplay

SOUL STORY

Who is quitting dogs today? Making them their sister?
Who is stretched out by a lampost sibling? Illuminated by ransom's note?

I was oblivious to pettiness until I saw its first handle: obey ignorance.
Stomach decisiveness. By that, this decision...no decision.

Let it be to gain all it can in one fetter...but if it be life,
let it attempt a failed recognition.

Let its thinker be the failure. My thinker is failure,
and I want to teach it how to move in this world.

Do you be or live?
To any the other wants.

To both these words, I fail to be.
When I am, but when not...

It is, as if alive.

WHAT IS ALTOGETHER ORDINARY

Solar planes have awakened in me
a most unusual happenstance—
to me and only me it appears
that the unexplained phenomena of the day
have somehow escalated, case in point:

On a hot summer day—
beached whales in search of their edge
find what appears to be
the edge of their water. Beached,
as horizontal accomplices to time,
they wait in the hope that the tide will find them.

Or else, a copier copies blank papers
with a code of symbols across the top of each blank page
—an unexplained source in the sweltering heat.
Or else, a planet in another galaxy
extracts heat from its sun when passing near—
edge becoming, in search of center.

...if I give you what I need, will you take what you want...

A sandwich order mistaken.
A missing page from a new book.
A traffic light stuck in the color of what moves.
The street sidewalk divided.
The air itself heat-waved—split vertically.
People melting while passing by, in the split...

I see them see me before they split—the asphalt of the city
drenched with solar flares, reaching out
through a horrendous science of light years,
encoupled in a temperate waltz through indecision—
an atmosphere bursting of heat and vision.

we are mountains of hype and dna
egos brushed with sun dapple
we are mere whispers of blood
sybillant monsters in paisley come

I was on my last legs, it was clear to me now.
But I wouldn't know until I was gone, that I was in that absolute territory
before you go—and no one else saw what I'd become
the rendered reach of this happening,
because it happened everyday to everyone at some point—
it was just my turn now.

I walked vertical in the haze
and imagined my apocalyptic glaze
as a private entrance into my ending—a gash into the gone.
A wound suspended in the smoldering heat, a trapped image torqued
in the concrete air. The gloom of snapshot captives, red-eyed natives
gestured in a frozen world, particular miscreants and emblems of doom
became apparent to me—where otherwise,
it'd be up to someone else to elevate the grime,
to highlight detritus into shadow,
to shove history into every wrinkle.

The day that happened yesterday
was an exact foreshadow of this movie I would see
in a few weeks—number one, number two…

I called this radio station for the title of a song that was playing.
The DJ told me what the song was, and the one before also.
Thanks I said, and hung up.
60 minutes later the DJ announces the song he has just played
is the same title he gave me an hour ago.
The song he just played, he hadn't played yet, when I called,
but was going to, but did he know that, when I first called?
Was he reading his playlist out of order, but this radio station
has no playlist and is programmed on intuition, and this song
was what I heard—and its title traveled
one hour ahead of its time continuum, its appointed time
to receive me in my ear, accelerated by the dimension
of an unformed solstice.

I had to catch my breath—I looked out the window,
my sightlines guided through heat by time.
From here the insects look like people,
and this window—a skin caught by light.

Had I heard what I thought I heard? Now or earlier?
Was he foreshadowing? Was I?
Did he or I hear what would play in one hour?
Reinterpreting what was heard with a particular ear towards
unexplained prophesy—foreshadowing space as illuminated by hearing.

...if I tell you what you want, will you take what you need...

voice mail message remains—hidden in voice box
discovered page appears—torn from old book
traffic light says walk—people don't
solar flares continue—to insist on my blindness

...if I show you what I need, will you give me what you want...

I am a planet equally aligned for desire or info—number two
number three...case in point—recent email:

> **"am using poem you sent 3 years ago for then defunt (sic) mag ...**
>
> **will debut momentarily need updated bio ...**
>
> **are you still living where you were will send copies ...**
>
> **hope all is well..."**

3 years has caught up to me
yet here I am, foreshadowing skin in the blistering heat.
3 years, selected parts of my life, who I was, what I was writing,
the *ago* of all those words—
has caught up to me, in a momentary thirst cylindrical by torment.
A sign of this end-space I find myself in.

Unusual phenomena have been heightened
by the mortal claim of this solar wind,
navigating through each crevice I leave unprotected.
3 years as a snapshot of desire.
A collection of what desire can do when surrounded by time.

If space is my accomplice to time, what parrallel to be in?
Where the eventful summary of *suddenly* is as current as *now*.

The season of lasting is gone
it is time to allow the air its split—to allow this body motion
between heat and illumined etherea
cresting the emboldened wave.

My ears are tuned to this snapshot —
from then to now, I see you
in the split.
The space between—where I've been,
mortal as rain.

VACANT SPEED

Cameo cloud
broached against
the neck of the world

Tower of milk
smoke against
the universe

Selfing necklace
chiseled
out of sky

Starts, how I'm I
isn't again
the falling grain

Grey has
beauty bombed out
by time

Slower by the point
it takes to make
it so

Vacant coloring
vacant speed
slower than anywhere

Locomotive sky
changing water
piston blue

Bracelet cloud
againsted by its
steam

Isn't this
falling, how I
against falling, pick up
speed

SPUTTERED SEEDSONG

The body gives / me body with / my body now
The fingers of / my hand are on / my fingers now
Guardians are / my fingers on / my hands now
Body breaks / my body wants / to body now
Creature tells / the creature wants / to draw ...oh
                    Scatter Day I'm calling you
                        what you used to be
                        a weekaday whisprell
                            wild and free ...oh

The body gives / me body when / it breaks now
The verbal is / the verbal in / the bod now
The bod is just / a boy inside / a bod now
The cloak is what / ignites me when / I look now
The brain will break / the brain into / the brain ...oh
                    float my hangline
                        glide this wash ...oh

The letter loses / letters in / the letters now
The lantern is / a lantern in / a sea now
The higher mind / will find itself / inside now
The injury / will answer what / is higher now
Intestines test / intestings what's / a test now
Againing is / my scattered enig / ma now
But tidy is / as tidy as / my drool ...oh

                cover my face—shower my spit
                    generation my dirt—gyration my blank slate
        bury me now—my chasm convinced
            feature me now—my face convinced
                    everytime—I see you
                I hold you—to the sound I own ... oh

I give you to / the panther in / my grace now
The sweated sun / embraces you / inside me now
The freedom is / a freedom / is inside now
Controling what / I / con / trol / now
Moving where / my arms can move / my arms ... oh
                Stand my legs
                        my lonesome rain
                dare to oak
                        my scattered spades ... oh

Sink me into / deep inside / my earth now
Ground me into / curve as / empty now
The man inside / the motion is / a man now
Roach me on / the back and I'm / left now
Wounding my light / as I wander ...
                    now wondering in wounded light

MIRROR METEOR

Pixie-dust infusion
shoots steady shock through incline—
is that crooked
or slyster meat tong, grabbing hold of night
so as not to pulse so bright past outcome

Pardon the excess—it's a point to make
that out of all this dirt
comes glass or shiny sheen
meant to gloss
over rough spots—let's moan and breathe

At one time, so that anything shattered
will sound pretty
I need to show how I love—sound and vision
if I sing and move to what I hear
and feel, just for you

Well, let's see if we can match
our limbs to the credible—or maybe the possible
let's play again, so that
you know what you're in for,
when you save your last dance for glass

How clutterdust of me—
and here's where I lose
my head over a star system,
a horny section
ten thousand years older than me

HORSES FOR THOMAS

Now
When there was nothing
The boy heard nothing

I feel different
I don't hear crunch and splak
When nothing happened
I used to hear crunch and splak

He was born
With explosions in his head
He thought it was normal
To hear the inside of your head
Cracking

UNWELLED

scalloped brain folds
grey ventricle skin
microscopic why

whyness bewills itself
whying into wellness
why a well of what

a will upon
a whip of whats
a why machine

to why at those woo-ers
wishing whacks at woe
becausing a cause of be

of is
of why be
cause

why
is the way of where
of will with when

why is my warning
my borrowed line
come to life

my wested way
my easted mast
why

is the sunhole
that flits me gregarious
questions me I

why is the flit
the orange byway
forcing unwords from
when

from why-hole
followed by
why is we

be-
witched by
when

HOW ABOUT

let's interupt liquid dancing
inner rupture redundancy
debased by diction banality
audiential sublimity
       let's react erupting cadence
       excuse my contextual lip
       my marsupial perimeter
       stabilized by your talkative lack o'color

> *witness*
> *be credit*
> *to shock*

> *I look wonderful*
> *for someone*
> *my type*

let's stare at the impolitic
I supposed to get me
color vision wiseass
I meant to say impolite
       some porous levels
       be love layers in loving pode
       this eager molting is culti physique
       religioning the bioloco socikal

> *I*
> *see*
> *life, c'mon*

man, don't

go

there

insipal limpshot rammed into moment
let's path up the paired redone
observed by the scittered tattered
those earth mudders who laser hello black into season
> who jester the non again with cornbone vornacular
> let's insert duende dexi into that molten lingua
> ripped open flumber how dumbness happens
> by reflux admission

> *be*

> *yur*

> *best name*

> *across*

> *yu*

> *other inguish*

in the interest of tim timbo
severating the hora attack let's lie
not to belong
but to collab the co-optum
> let's disconnex blockage from
> defamed intellooneries harnished by sugary erasure
> wordering extendaramery you know, let's just
> impulse the prominent

THE LIMITLESS LIMINAL

one day leaks ... zero zero
the other ... obscurant eyehole
permanent fissure ... twenty two two
for a man in touch with leaky leaky... soupy soupy
me dia ... zip zip
some hermetic structure [what expression]... plus plus
moving away from [papa patria] ... libro bro
rigorous page ... expansion in [cooler to squeak] the code
other sites [flippy flip] legitimate ...
[what is] expression
[investigation into] ... clip clop ... [others]
[told you] pops or peeps ... yo yo yo
what interference [hummina hummina]
into the general [static] cultural ... uno [the mimeo me]

MERELY A POET

THAT ONE, is a poet for all poets
AH, *then I would suppose*
to be an edwin for all edwins
OH, then there is only one of you
you are being one for
AH, *I am one of me*
but one is too many for all
OH, then how can this one be for all
when that one is truly for truly's sake
Which one?
It isn't a which or a what but a be
HMMPF, *an ending for all endings*
UMMPF, to be a poet for poets
is a mere suppose
BLECHH, *you covered suppose in an earlier poem*
YUCHH, but no one heard it
ARGH, *they say a poem is heard when it is written*
ERGH, then I have heard my entire life
as it happens
HOOOPHA, *a mere one, an entire suppose,*
this has been . . .
WAIT, are you implying an ending?
AHA, *a being*
OHO, now there is a poem
OOOOH, *an ending*
AHHHH, where there are so many to choose from

VAYACOM.CULO

Zooming to Creatia—onna speed boat
Flumes of white behind us—Speed demon pastors
Zloom along—Matriar'tactic Adrianen Sunset Wucla
Let's go shwooned wet licks—slicked Hadism
Enoughism...of this-ism; woe-ism

TVism; on boatism—shows view of where we've been-ism
face front—direction of travel;
face view; of rear wake; imagine
if we had; tiny monitor; facing us; inside eyeglasses
with view; from Butt Camera; showing
rear ass of trail we leave; imagine that...huh?

Video on MTV of ass shaking; where what's shook
is Behindex—squeezed on tiny monitor
shoved in eyeglass frame; walking trying to look
while looking trying to walk; who would you run into
while looking where you shouldn't...

> (whistle) Oops!
> Oh, Hi...Hey what are you doing!
> Oh, just watching my ass while I walk.
> Oh, that why you're neck like that!
> Oh, it look strange?
> No, you remind me of Behinder Troll!
> Oh, I have all the collection!
> You do?
> Yes, even the one with pink tuft out of green ass.
> That one is the rare one!
> But, I have!

Yes, you say! And now ...you feel pinch?

Yes, with all kind gumbot!

Oh! Well, I go.

You judge only as go.

I fall you eye-head, go BOOM! Ha Ha!

Ha Ha, good fiend! Well, my continue walk goes ... BUUUMP! OH, hi!

Hello, you must be Ass Folke!

Again? It shows?

Yes, your neck.

Oh!

You are behinding with video stucks in butt wad!

Ha ha ...and you?

I am fine, have hairdo of pubal chest!

I see.

Bifocal Crack Chgeek, how prestty!

Pretty!

Well, it hank. Go now!

Thanks, you have Stainless T-Spot!

Oh, one of each.

Flat Brick-Chak? Boy, the full bloomer!

Behinder Troll?

Ass Check!

Bye now!

I see! (whistling) Gorge Coke is Zoom Pock ...

    Facey, Pimple Trip-Noy? BOOOOMP?

    Oh, I dawn see who I ...PUNNNK!

    Oh, I own hair twisty whip ...Fluff-Nut Touché!

    Behinder Ass!

    Oh, so goo!

CATALAN BONANZA TRANSLATION

(or "an attempt to translate a bonanza episode in catalan using imagined spanish")

<u>Scene 1: Late afternoon, Catalan Ben Cartwright's home office, facing a moral dilemna, he sits at a table discussing strategy with Catalan Bonanza Guy Dressed In Black:</u>

-Well, I hate to eat your farina … but …

-It's okay, I don't have secrets!

-The world BITES me?

-NO!

-Very well, EAT the blue dress! (pause) I'm thinking about our days …

I was sure I was … pushing you!

-How have you changed?

-YES?

-hmmm … first time for blue hair.

-To die and to know?

-I'm sorry, it's easier to pray … (stands and puts cowboy hat on) … later!

-My dress … (Ben hands him a box)

-The shaw? … (Ben sheepishly grins)

-Okay!

(music builds, cut to outside, Catalan Ben on his horse, riding away)

Scene 2: Late afternoon town saloon,
Catalan Mary is flirting with this episode's handsome rascal

-Will you kiss on my rats, Mary?

-Astrologically?

-You're a special deal ...natural... Mary?

-There is fever on your opinion!

-I can't...Mary...but don't tell us!

(music builds as they kiss, cut to closeup of bartender's jaw)

Scene 3: Saloon at night, Catalan Bonanza Guy Dressed In Black
playing cards with this episode's villain

-Why, these are cards of love! Show me your . . . itinerary!!!!! Ha Ha Ha Ha Ha

(demonic laughter,cut to commercial)

Scene 4: Kitchen at night, Catalan Ben Cartwright's house,
Catalan Mary is dressing a wound on Catalan Little Joe's
forehead as Catalan Hoss looks on

-You live here?

-People have women!

-Thank you!

-Space & time have altered your fly ...

-Your trap!

-Pushy aren't you?

-You rabbit!

-How stringy and mousey you are ...

    (Catalan Little Joe whimpers in pain)

-Suck the goat, brave!

-You, I don't know why, have a misfit nose! Hmmm ... Child of No No?

-Don't tell me ... I'M SMALL?

    (they both nod)

-GET OUT OF HERE!

-BUT, MEN ARE BOYS IN MARCH!

-Push me ... you, you ...

    (there is a struggle)

-WHERE IS THE RAFFLE WHEN YOU SLEEP?

    (fists flying, Catalan Little Joe leaves)

-(Catalan Mary yelling) DON'T MENTION THE CRUSHED DRESS!

    (turning to Catalan Hoss) ... Hello ...

    (Catalan Hoss surprised but sheepishly, returns her stare,
    fade to commercial)

Scene 5-epilogue: Sunset, outside, Catalan Mary and Catalan Hoss
face each other, a horse between them

-Hello...

-I breathe deeply to imply that I miss you.

-Yes, I feel it.

(they mount the horse)

-Crush me, and I'm happy!

(end theme, credits)

surfacenoise

SLIPPED CURVE

danger is the birth of angles
shazz'd; lettroin; marved; eld
enticing; the shape beckons
rip in sky; throat opens

when ungorged; a curve
features formless, out of reshaped voweletter
yellow vegas bundesbähn
welcome to the four-eyed boys

zizz'd; mreckt; taon; vevved
shell-shocked leather-clad; mad punkt
takes over soundpakt; easier to listen
if you take away; fear; peligrøtz

lover street; luuversträsse
jammed mother's vilk-kummen; mira
the minister's house; shadowblakt
by nicht-shak; danger is the birth of angles

geo-momo; retric-meutschland
the birth of danger is *ingles*
curve un-complished; comfort word
anglish saxo; birth of dango

finding the approaching; storm approached
patriarch-tactic; tac-toe tolerant
skinned by scarlet; stripes and stars
o ruby riff; o long ago

alexanderplatz; loco
boricua; das chicaletz .
sank pakt; acht-man
sleeper leaps; a million sans omen

glowning echo; what is free; is not the feather
that is feathered but; the feather
torqued horizon; foontakt remora
crossed crag; gleamed; by curve just missed

what is danger pinched; nasal-ostroso
look; more graffiti by esl punks
graphis on danger; wall to wall
"look more" it sez; call attention

to calling; nasal punkt?
no; esl; oh; messers
lander ünd platz; einer poesie
existen der rim of der; planetun

tight birth; nicht night
enticing; no?
the shape
that beckons

THE THEORIST HAS NO SAMBA!

there is a new instantism > a language of tangent =
tanguage > ambient funguage > there is a modern path
>invented through accidental spontaneity + of mock
language sport = fractured intelligentsillys > there
are sage athleticists + important children farmed out
to the furthest reaches of nowness > ... > ... >

I propose a New Instantism. Take spontaneousness out
of the ether and smack it into the throes of the wild
screaming bastard maggot that IS poetry! I propose a
New NEWness, where we refuse to comply by the aged
fumblings of mere MEANING and instead descend into
mere HEARING! I instigate a NEW failure of
listening ... so we may one day walk hand in hand with
our own ears and say ... THANK THE MIGHTY LOUD
THAT I MAY THANK THE MIGHTY LOUD THAT
I MAY THANK THE MIGHTY LOUD! I have
a NEW Instantaety, a modern NEWness, a
post NOWism ... I have a fear ... of hiding this fear,
instead ... I choose a revelry of failure, an opportune
dimentia into the song of my pacifism.

Let's say we level expectation with implied tension.
The instant doubt appears, possibility appears next to it as a window.
What was thought to have clarity is now diffused by possibility.
Is possibility the goal ... or only the instant before doubt?

The New Instantists will allow possibility room to
doubt itself...inventing a paranoia into the sleepless
monster that is this bastard maggot poetry. The New
Instantist will know that it takes a flat surface to
iron out procedure, that a wrinkled pair of favorite
pants will match an equally wrinkled ass...and mind.
That no matter how just or unjust the outcome...the
New Instantist will always be blamed for what has just
happened! Occurence...being the signpost
for all things instant.

To what is now
And what is never then
To what has been
And what will never now
To things all thinging
And soon all soon'ing
To what is now
Instantly now

E-MAN'S PROCLAMATION

if we the people were as funny as you say, then
we the people would laugh at us the laughers!
let me now talk the talk said filled of THE
since I will then be obliged to walk this walk I did
once, walking the walk led me
nowhere! what is the deal of this walk that people say
you must walk only because you have talked
what they, the people, have said is talk!

I never asked my talk to be called THE talk,
why enshrine levitation with needless THE'ing?
there is too much THE *for* the people! if we the people
did all the talking why is there no walking?
why do WE the they, or THEM the us, stay happy
remote folk-trolls, crouched before screen
flicking entrails of america's collective people bargain?
and while we're at it, {as WE as can be}, let me now say

the saying, as a preface pre-facing, what follows,
implying following! if we the followers
were as noisy as you say we are...although here I may be
implying footings in mouthings by way of unfounded
findings and all manner of those'ings...then we the followers
would allow us the followed to be, one and
the same...making us be the we you say we are!
at this moment of WE, the people have slept that the sleep,

ate that the food, thought this the thought,
shot that the shat, seen that the seen, helped that the helpless,
starved that the starving, killed this the world,
less that the home, fly that the bird does, butter that the fly,
feather that the tar does, biggie up the size, the skin, the in you're in
and so on the SO'ing...so, how did THE get so belonging?
they say my we belongs to me,
and because I have talked the talk, I am now on my way

to my walk, as noisy as the noisers would say
I am...if we the people could hear them

NORICUA BBQ SUMMIT *(for Libertad, Monxo, & Urayoan)*

Noricuaaaaaa, no-no-no-no-no-no, no-no-no-no
a, e, i, o, no...bobo, bobo, bobo, bobo

Soy Noriqueño
 Soy Noricua
Son Noriqueño
 Son of Noricua

Hijo de mentiraso
 Mira me dueña
Hijo de mentiro-soso
 Tira man-te-caca

Chibo sa miqua
 Pico cabaña
Sapa pa tista
 Sfis sfis sfis sfis sfis sfis sfis...{noqui}

LOS ROC GODS – DISPIERTA – EN LA FERTILA-UERZA!
LOS DIOS DE PIEDRA – WAKE UP – IN THE FERTILE-FORCE!

Oh mano, los rocos son sano de fuerza,
Oh tierra, mis labios son locos de fuerza,
Oh no-no, mis labios son lucky, de hijos, mijos, niños
Oh foto, me sono son buena, son llena de cositas

Si, ver buenza
 Siga, si mienta
Sin verguenza
 Seer, sage, bien Buena

WIN! WIN! M●NEY! M●NEY!
ESTA CHICA! MUCH● B●NITA!

Yo, I'm way outta mi buena
Super Way, Super Bueno, Super BuenBuenzamiga

I'm outta mi boca with grief, see
Mami got snared by belief, *oui*
Papi got tied up by ritmo, and me
Uh-uh, my *who* be, *be*?, no-no? si-si-si-si, si-si-si-si ...{noqui}

Soy Noriqueño
    Soy Noricua
Son Noriqueño
    Son of Noricua

Mi-ra{-ra}, la-la-tino diva{-va}, takes a turn,
    for the mysterioso{-so-so}
O-ye{-ye-ye}, the scary Edgar Allen Poemo{-so-so}
    sings a mucho largo Bori-cuo{-cuo-cuo}
For the Presi-dodo{-dodo-dodo}

Yo-yo{-yo-yo}, back off on the Noricua BBQ
No grill ala George Foreman, no heat, no meat, no you{-you-you}
No steak, chicken, hamburger, fries
No hot dog rolls, no bunions, no escarole, no funions
Haci-chuela? no sauce, Hace-pesto? mano-festo{-to-to-to}

There is no grill in the Noricua BBQ
No cooking required, no people, no you
We're all here waiting for, no you
Being we without, being you

WE'RE ALL THE NOJENTE – ALL THE NOTIME
AT THE NORICUA BBQ – BEING Q IS BEING YOU!

Mira esso, mira puro
    No ai esso, no hay puro
The Mocker Spaniel, es el perro mas puro
    The No-quer Spaniel es el puro mas perro
Bow wow-wow-wow-wow-wow-wow-W●W!

The Island Vieques, es la isla mas linda
    The Island No-quies, es la linda mas isla
Pow-pow-pow-pow-pow-pow-pow-POW!

The People Taino, es la jente mas antes
    The People No-ino, es la antes mas jente
La-la-la-la-la-la-la-la-LA-TINY-TINO-LAND!

There is no noise in the Noricua BBQ
We are noisy, without noise
Los neighbors who aren't there
Gimme nothing in return
Noricua no tiene vecinos
Gimme nothing to return to

Something Something, Something Something
Something Something – keep it down, bro

Tiene Boron-Cocoron
　　Sono Quoriqa
Neither Noricua
　　Nor-Ricua be!

Es el ritmo, ai mismo
　　No es ritmo, es polit-mo
Estes ritmo, no es ritmo
　　O es estes, ritmo nada
No me nada, hasta algo
　　Si ai algo, no hay nada

Noricua en mi No-razon
Noricua en mi Relampagon
Noricua en mi No-uerpo'n
No, is noise my noise
Nada, is my noise, no … is No-i-s-e

No, is
Es, si

CORRECTION

I like to see; *next question*—have the chief;
I want to BE chief, *if I can*
I've always been interested; *I'd like that*
to be, *if I can*; in destination, pretty much the same
also, the bottom; young ones who work hard; THERE
I consider myself—*if I can*, yep...
harmonius; born; can't fake it, *the next line, I mean*...but
I would never; *wait—that wasn't*; now
what I DIDN'T prove; wasn't clear—right here
I could...*if I could FIRST*, okay fine; let's do...
barely; then the last line—*anyone could put*;
well then, *the LAST line*, going down
to a different, *how about this—two words*;
ONE and SELF, *with some enthusiam*; heroism—
wait...*h*...*e*... *r*...; actually, *I'm sorry*
that MIGHT be right; and possess, *my own—I*, each man
and where it goes; is where that was,
it should say; a *man* and *unman*; I don't
know if, by now—you've; *what I would do is*...recognize some aspect;
if I am; it's part—*of*—or—*god*, or *the godecese*
involved; *that's right*—halfway through, take it out; *this is professional*
etcetera; I didn't care, *and so on*—should we speak; THAT would be...or
that; AND that...take out; THAT; *I'd like to feel*
spiritly; that, giving you THAT, have—has;
only then, the THAT should...*once, as the only thing*; I; THE
only thing; *should be a space*, should there BE a space
under *unman*; WHO is able or not—with enthusiam,
two words—I think so;

PEDRO'S INVITATION

so listen, I'll call you 'cuz I have
your number and I swear you should meet
someone, right? I mean that person I told you about?
like 2 years ago? should be the next person
you meet that's a non-human impossibility
I know, but what I'm saying is that
someone like that, would like to meet you
or someone like you, or the chance to have
a phone conversation with the essence of
what you're about right? so listen
I have your phone number, I swear
you gotta meet this person I'll call you, right
'cuz look, I got your phone number
and like 2 years ago I told you about this
person right? I got your phone number
right? I'll call you look do me a favor,
write your phone number down for me
I mean I got your number but write it down
'cuz you gotta meet this person, right?
look I'll call you 'cuz there's this person
you gotta meet and this number works right?
so good, okay listen, so like, 2 years ago...

VIOLATED OVAL: A Conversation with Orion

-How's it goin'?
Ah ...I lost my pad—

-How?
I got kicked out—

-When?
After a 9-month seclusion—By a momentary secretion—
I'm a yolk, see—
I'm a constant egg—And no incubator exists to hatch me—
I've just realized that—
And I'm happy I've realized that—No daddy exists—
To lay his rump on me—
To allow my rupture—I'm an unfertilized egg—
Totally content—Always in here—
Never worried about—Feeling its scrawny neck—
Out the hole of my crack—
I'm never to BE cracked—There exists no ax or hatchery—
With the power to perform this—
Greybeard Shylock—Me & Ginsberg—
I'm an elephant with tusks—
From here to Ginsberg—A Rhinocerous—
A One-Horned Shylock—
A Unicorn for Ginsberg—Or perhaps just a eunuch—

-O.K, See ya later...
Whether I see you or not—Is irrelevant—
I may choose to speak—
You may choose to ignore me—I am happy—
With this arrangement—

BIO-RODENT-ORIOLE

Began the year by seeing the rat uncheesed,
freedom is a destiny drubbed in bloomers.
Soily clothed emperor's bum,
nudely chewed by the anals of reversism
afooted by numerology,
an alternative January appears.

Calendrical cheesebombs
in the upside-down year.
Left elbow throbs with leftover maturity,
last part of me still holding first part...know m'sayin?

My inner chick's a gosling
spreading unfound winglets, by way
of pain, in said left limb joint.
I arrive to the offering, nobly beheaded
by the waiting throng—annointed by despair—rat says:

> Welcome, and make sure you support the mob
> better yet—reject everything...it's better off!

> To which I respond:
> I've come to see how the other half lives.

> Better you should see them die—says rat —
> same difference! I had once a healthy diet, fluidity
> composed a major portion of my day, no swine.
> A mere utterance of the bovine sally—was enough
> to last a season, afraid of no path!

This newfound approach to my tattered jubilee
lasted a composite of 40 days—in homage
to that twin-beast keeper floating his misguided barge.
As a matter of fact, the only vice I missed—dare I drone,
the one which claimed this broken bod back to its
previous owner ... was writing!

Yes, I'd completely given up the sword
when I started eating healthy; physically, I was magnificent!
Tip top, the entire cadaver—a destiny braved; mentally...

I had grown an extra femur—an extended weasel
protruding, from the rear of my intestine
through the skin and out the chickawa!
Although I cared for this uninvited guest as I would
my own grail, the 3 am feedings grew tiresome.
I decided it was time to relinquish control
and carnivate this herbivore—by way of pen.

I now stand before you complete—trashed
and unhealthy!

This event proceeded, without me, a mere
eight days ago. I am currently unhealthy
and writing—as opposed to a past state!
I believe in a life that exists presently, I am
implicit in motion, and I've yet to welcome
the new year. All these things can be rectified ...
knowingly—I refuse!

PSYCHE-OUT PSUEDONYMROD

I put the word where I didn't
think I would but that didn't happen
till I picked it up and saw how light it was
how agile I can flex it upside itself and see
the belly of it Oh it's too heavy better
leave it right where I found it where I seen it
first Oh it broke was trying to lift it
by that part and it just broke
right off its context right off the place
where it had its most meaning right
where I thought I knew what I was
trying to say by saying it once
I seen it pump out m'mouth and land in front
it wasn't my word at all but a
cinammon—*know'm sayin'*

THE FUTURE MRS. TORRES

ENIGMISTICA ! THE FUTURE MRS. TORRES !

AN ACCIDENT OF GRAND ELOQUENCE !

INTER NOCHE REALE ! BELLE ! ENIGMISTICA

! (TV , CANALE 5) GRANDE ! UNBELIEVABA

! CONTESTO DI EDDIE ! SULTANO ! UN

BELLE VIE ! D' AVANTE ! THE FUTURE

MRS. TORRES ! ANGORA ! OGGLE PONTO

FELICI - CITA ! FLAT ICOLA ! TORNQUEST ?

AVIVA ! VINTI DAINTY - NEXT ! SEGUNDO !

COMPAY ! ENIGMISTICA ! THE FUTURE

MRS. TORRES ! LL GRANDE SCENA !

(TV, CANALE VIÇENTE) LIPPI - COW - BOY !

AY YAY ! NUOVA RAG ! PANCHA DRAW !

UNA ONE ! L' EX BARECHEST - PROMETTO

PER ATTACHEMENT ! PETTO HA ? E !

ENIGMISTICA ! MARIE DE MRS. E !

FUTURO DE CHAPPOS ! SONO ANCHE ?

NO - SONO FLACO ? AH ! LEGANTO !

ATLETICA ! UNBELIEVABA ! PARTITE !

ENIGMISTICA ! THE FUTURE MRS.

'ORRRRRRRRRRES !

LADY WHACK-JOB MEET SEÑOR THANK-YOU

MADAME IN-THE-SHIT-OF-MY-SERIOUSNESS *meet* MR. IT'S-ABOUT-TO-GET-FUNKY-IN-HERE

SEÑORITA SUPERSTAR *meet* MR. LOUSY-ACCENT

MONSIEUR JESUS *meet* LADY LA-LA-TOO-BAD

LITTLE MISS GOT-SOME-FAT-DADDY-CASH *meet* SIR SWEATS-THRU-HIS-SHIRT-AND-CALLS-IT-PROGRESS

MR. TRANSPORTS-RADIOACTIVE-WAH-WAH-WITH-HIS-OVERGROWN-SHPLORT-MOBILE *meet*

SENIOR OFFICER HOLD-YOU-BY-THE-SCUM-OF-MY-DEDICATED-SHITHOLE

MR. DID-I-MENTION-SHIT-ALREADY *meet* MRS. YES-YOU-DID-AND-YOUR-NUBS-ARE-SHOWING

MRS. PASS-MY-BOREDOM-BY-STARING-DOWN-YOUR-ZITS *meet* MRS. PUMPY-JUMP-THE-SHHHH-MEISTER

PRINCE FACSIMILE-MONSIEUR *meet* ASS PASSENGER EXPOSÉ

BROTHERS AIN'T-NO-SPRING-CHICKEN & CHEW-CUD *meet* THE FAMILY FOOSBALL:

MOLDY, MONTY, MURDY, SHASHA & LITTLE PLIÉ

COUNT SHUT-YER-TRAP *meet* BARON VON MAKE-ME

LITTLE GET-OFF-THAT-DAMN-CELLPHONE *meet* COUSIN SHOVE-IT

MRS. EXPECTS-A-HANKY-AFTER-THAT-NOSE-JOB? *meet* SEÑORITA ASK-ME-IF-I-CARE

MR. DUE-TO-A-DISPUTE-AMONG-THE-STAFF *meet* MRS. PICK-UP-THE-COURTESY-PHONE-DAMMIT

KING TIE-DIE-NANCY *meet* PHAROAH NEVER-GOT-LAID

SEÑORITA SAYONARA *meet* MRS. MILKY-BROWN-STUFF-COMING-OUT-HER-PIZZA

MRS. OH-PLEASE-BORE-US-WITH-YOUR-VAGUE-WISDOM *meet* MONSIEUR SELF-IMPORTANTÉ

MR. TOO-OLD-TO-BE-SITTING-THERE-WITH-YOUR-FLY-OPEN *meet* MR. BREATHE-MY-FANCY-HISTORY

KNIGHT OF THE MASTER ROUND TABLE YOU-GOTTA-BE-KIDDING *meet* CHIEF OF STAFF I'M-OUTTA-HERE

MACRO TELL-ME-ANOTHER-LIE-AND-I'LL-SPRAY-YOU-WITH-MY-SHEEPSKIN *meet*

VEGAN PICKS-THE-LINT-OFF-HER-BREAST-WITH-HER-MANTRA

MRS. L.E.D.-DISPLAY *meet* MR. MARBLES-IN-YOUR-PANTIES

MADEMOISELLE PLASTIC-BAG-NIGHTMARE *meet* MONSIEUR IT'S-ABOUT-TIME

YOUNG LOVERS QUICK & DRAW *meet* PORNSTARS LONG & HARD

MR. RECORDS-EVERYTHING-IN-SIGHT *meet* MRS. PUT-THAT-THING-AWAY-OR-I'LL-CUT-YOUR-ARMS-
OFF-AND-SHOW-YOU-WHAT-THE-WORLD-LOOKS-LIKE-WITHOUT-YOUR-CONSCIENCE

MADEMOISELLE HIDING-BEHIND-YOUR-MAKE-UP-ONLY-MAKES-YOUR-STINK-PROUD *meet*

SONNY BOY BEATS-OFF-FOR-DINNER-WHEN-HE-CAN'T-AFFORD-TO-PAY-CAUSE-THAT'S-HOW-THEY-
DID-IT-BACK-IN-THE-DAY

HOMEBOY I-KNOW-YOU-LUCKED-INTO-THAT-RHYME *meet* FLYGIRL SO-WHAT *friend of*

SUCKER MC SHUT-YOUR-FOOL-HEAD-OR-I'LL-SPRINKLE-YOUR-ROOFIES-WITH-SPANKY-PUCK

MR. NEEDS-NO-DEODERANT-BECAUSE-HE'S-FOREIGN *meet* MADAME OPINIONS-OUT-HER-MONKEY

LADY MAKE-OUT-SESSION *meet* PRINCE BUSHY-EYEBROWS

SEÑORITA LIP-FACE *meet* SEÑOR TINY-TOO-TIGHT

MRS. BADLY-NEEDS-SOME-SUN *meet* MR. CAN'T-AFFORD-TO-WORK-'CUZ-THAT'LL-MESS-WITH-HIS-FREEDOM

MADAME POINTS-OUT-OTHER-PEOPLE'S-DEFECTS *meet*

PRESIDENT HIT-IN-THE-FACE-WITH-A-2-BY-4-AND-STILL-GETS-SOME-WANK-ON-HIS-WINK

MR. PUSHES-A-ROCKSTAR-OFFSTAGE *meet* MISS PISS-OFF-THE-BOURGEOISIE-WITH-HER-ACTIVIST-BOOKEEPING

MADEMOISELLE LOOK-WHO'S-SUDDENLY-MISS-AVAILABLE *meet*

MR. LOOK-WHO'S-SUDDENLY-SEÑOR-EMOTIONAL

MOVIE STAR NEEDS-A-TRAINING-BRA-TO-COVER-HIS-G-SPOT *meet*

MOVIE STAR COVERS-HER-GRAY-WITH-THE-COLOR-OF-SHAME

SPORTS COLUMNIST ONE-LAME-JOKE *meet* RESIDENT ALIEN I-GET-IT-ALREADY

LORD CARRIES-HIS-GUITAR-BY-THE-NECK-LIKE-A-GEEK *meet* LADY BLOWS-HER-FLUTE-LIKE-A-PRO

LITTLE BOY-BIG-HEAD *meet* LITTLE MISTER-VOMIT-BAG

MADEMOISELLE KNOWS-A-THING-OR-TWO-ABOUT-SLEEPING-WITHOUT-MONEY *meet*

MONSIEUR GETS-IT-WHEN-NO-ONE'S-LOOKING

MISTER EGGS-IN-HIS-BEARD *meet* MRS. PAIN-IN-THE-ASS

MR. FIVE-O-CLOCK-SHADOW *meet* MR. THREE-MINUTE-MAN

SHORT ORDER CHEF THOUSAND-MILE-CLUB *meet* FOUR DOOR SALESMAN DUCK-L'ORANGE

MR. CUTS-LUMBER-TO-PISS-OFF-HIS-LOAN-OFFICER *meet* SEÑORA ASBESTOS-COWHEAD

MR. PULL-YOUR-SHORTS-TIGHTER-SO-WE-CAN-GET-A-LOOK-AT-WHAT-MAKES-YOU-SO-SPECIAL *meet*

MADAME GIMME-A-REASON-TO-DIAL

MISS WHAT'S *meet* MISS YOUR *friend of* MR. PROBLEM

MR. AUTOMATIC-MORON *meet* MRS. UNLIKELY-EVENT

MISTER HUNG-LIKE-A-STALLION *meet* MISTER PEES-LIKE-A-RACEHORSE

SIR LACK-OF-SELF-COMPOSURE-DOING-WHAT-HE-THINKS-HE-LIKES-CUZ-HE-THINKS-THAT'S-WHAT-

YOU-WANT *meet* LITTLE LORD PUSH-UP-BRA

TRAPEZE RACONTEUR GIVES-IT-UP-TO-WHOEVER-BUTTERS-HER-LUBE-JOB *meet*

PROFESSIONAL BULLY WIPES-IT-WITH-WHATEVER'S-HANDY

MR. WHAT-PLANET-ARE-YOU-FROM *meet* MRS. WHO-DIED-AND-MADE-YOU-BOSS

and finally

LITTLE MISS-PERFECT *meet my banker* MR. SUCK-OFF

INERT PLUG

cb blurb wasteland
obscuratta
   got mad storytellers
shadowless shriker
   who look in
the yu by yu
   before out
seeing to see
   by dewdrop dysfunction
tell me a story
   by human creation
but start by the telling
   perfected as reject
tell me the picture
   what toll the teller
but bell the external
   nonhuman perfecture
foam me yur mirror
   genuwine artifice
but lie
   better leave
yur point
   when it yells
the guess
   gone
wobscured material

one letter
for mockstice
   key won't lock
artist of material
   til yu turn
reflects
   had yu to lose yu
porous invention
   is what moves
what would be
   yu
sayso
   goes far
logos in me-time
   does more with little
algorhythmic totem
   shock yu slow me
sifting connection
   show me yu pigment
in calm yu comb
   yur backdrop intention
yur bone
   yur instant prevention
yur coxlick
   yur brikabak
yur dome

ELDER DUBB

titty wainscott **n' all th'droppin's**

uvncle as uvula **wrinkled n' flat**

shove deceased corners **inna y' face**

older than I **witta dress f'courtsey**

a grunted pisser - proudly **coloratura n' cockatiels**

a preach on your son **wizened by wi(d)th**

by your girth **by y' pluggs y' falange**

yer dome **grayered n' blast(er)ed**

out of sync **t' mitty caloree**

noisy subtitle **t' elegance**

GOOD MORNING MR. PHELPS

The Baker has made only 10 croissants this morning, instead of his usual dozen. The villagers get angry when they discover that one of these prized croissants has been given to a visiting foreigner as a welcome gesture. Most surprising since over time, the villagers had come to consider foreigners *foreign* and had signed a pact whereby caring for themselves first was ritual not courtesy. However this gifted croissant was an anti-croissant—lacking the usual flakiness and fluff—as this morning's batch had not been baked with the expertise of the others, which was due to the Baker's rush in leaving town that morning.

It goes back to last year, when he missed the boat for his vacation. The next boat was a week away, meaning he would miss the birth of a prized goat on the mainland that afternoon— which he was to hear about by way of the Cobbler. Who, having missed the same boat, had walked across the ocean in his newly invented concrete boots, while breathing through a thin reed which broke the water's surface, which then enabled the Cobbler to reach the shore in time for a light snack of melon and goat cheese—and then for the birth of the prized goat. The Cobbler, having a keen sense of drama, would often snack on what he was about to witness.

The Cobbler and Baker had their stores on the same corner and were always competing for customers, which was never understood because shoes and bread were as different as feet and butter. No matter, what began as a minor disagreement had escalated over the years—a rivalry encouraged by the villagers, as it provided much in the way of entertainment since there was nothing else to do in town.

After the goat episode, the Baker was furious and vowed never to let the Cobbler get the upper hand again. Throughout the following year, they embarked upon a vicious verbal campaign against each other, to the delight of the villagers. Incorporating a modest budget for posters, they would each outdo the other in terms of vulgarity and visual appeal. Costly production techniques were continually improved upon, these posters became collector's items and the year was entitled "Concrete Perio" in honor of the concrete shoes and the era they gave rise to.

"Concrete Perio" established many artists as innovators of vulgarity, crossing the center of what many believe to be a historic moment in the telling of the *first half* of this story. And that, is why there are only 10 croissants today.

-The floor is now open to questions. *Yes...*

-*You have croissant crumbs all over your mouth...*

-Actually I was mugged. *Yes...*

-*And what is that in your hair...*

-Shoes and Butter. *Yes...*

-*But you have a piece of napkin on your nose...*

-They took both croissants. *Yes...*

-*I thought you only got the one...*

-There was a sale. *Yes...*

-*I like the first story better...*

Ah, well then. The acceptance of this newly aestheticized vulgarity was especially important to the *second half* of this story. Having suceeded in surrounding even the most vulgar announcement with highly developed graphic displacements of organic phrasing, the decorative aspect of "Concrete Perio" gave way to a more refined concentration of artists within the region—allowing an insult ground to flourish in an atmosphere of unparallelled vulgarity.

This well-crafted excess eventually attracted seekers of artistic liberation eager to voice anarchy's stranglehold on society's dish-pan government fired up against the mephisto wisdom of a tightly-knit community suffocated by its uniquely bull-headed soap-water ideology via an unparralleled lack of privacy cooked up by the rubbings of wrong-way participants led astray by liberty.

"Concrete Perio" Bakers and Cobblers were now accepted, not just within the island but on the mainland as well. At first as curiosity *chauvres*, but more recently as true progenitors of an artform unexpected to matter as much as it did PP (pre-Perio). Rather, it has—*still*, within the thin-reed public who, *to this day*, continue the practice of walking underwater wearing shoes of concrete, while breathing through their newly acquired penetration.

-Some tea?

-I'd love some!

[CHART EXPLANATION: *with no chart, using dance gestures:* IN LIEU OF CHART]

The Baker leaves to catch his boat—the dough rises rapidly and incorrectly— the anti-croissant is born. Here you can see where the foreigner arrives and where the town council has voted to expatriate the visitor—however on account of the rampant vulgarity running . . . rampantly, the message is miscommunicated. The messenger is so insulted by such . . . insultation, that the prized croissant is given to the foreigner—the hated *foreign* foreigner, out of spite. To this day, no one has heard from the Cobbler and there *may be* foul play involved.

[NEWSCASTER EXPLANATION: *with no camera, monotone voice, shoulders steady, stare straight into no camera, use head movements synchronized with pencil, underscoring capitalized key points:* IN LIEU OF NEWSCAST]

UnFORtunately, there was NO goat born ON this DAY. The BAKER grew inCENSED at having waited a FULL YEAR to CATCH his BOAT in reTURN for letting his DOUGH rise early. Upon his reTURN, he imMEdiately gave RISE to aNOther MOVEment, a new ORDER to FOllow. One that would PALE in comPARISon. This was to BE his SWAN song to the DAYS of BUTTER.

[VISUAL EXPLANATION: *with photos of the same man, wearing a different haircut for each character:* IN LIEU OF INTEREST]

The manifesto was to appear in a monthly letter published by *this* man, the Farmer. The Baker, now disguised as *this* man, the Butcher, set out to remove any knowledge of the Cobbler's family, and to *this* day no one has been found. We believe *this* man, the Fisher, *this* couple, the Twins, and ...those two over there, are involved. But not those two leave them alone, they don't even know we're looking.

As usual if any members of your organization are caught, we will disavow of any information leading to their capture. This story has self-destructed by now ...good luck Jim.

[present tape recorder and croissant on a plate, play "Mission Impossible" theme, eat croissant, wipe mouth, leave podium]

BOTTLE O' CHUTNEY

Well, (sigh) Paul can't come
Well, (sigh) Paul can't come
                    You can havhave a concush-have a concussion!
Let him come!
                    Cussion!
Let him come!
Let him c-c-c-come!
Paul can't come
            Let him come!
Paul can't come
            Let him come!
Paul can't come
            Let him come!
Paul can't come
            Let him come!
Paul can't come
can't come can't come can't come can't come
            Let him come
Well! Well!

All this for a bottle o'chutney huh?
Aieeeee
            Take it, huh? Just Take it, huh? Just just
            just just just (hmmmmm) take it!

[Aieeeee] all this for a bottle o'chutney huh?
[Aieeeee] all this for a bottle o'chutney huh?
[Aieeeee] all this for a bottle o'chutney huh?
[Aieeeee] all all all all all all all all all
[Aieeeee] all this for a bottle o'chutney huh?

Bottle o'chutney, huh?
Bottle o'chutney, huh?
Bottle o'chutney, huh?
Bottle o'chutney, huh?
Aieeeee] all all all all all all all all all

Paul can't come

Aieeeee] all all all all all all all all all

Let him come!

Aieeeee] all all all all all all all all all

Let him Let him Let him

Aieeeee] all all all all all all all all all

Come! [hmmmmmm] Well!

Aieeeee] all all all all all all all all all

I'll do I'll do anything
Let him come!
I'll do I'll do anything to come!
[hmmmmmmmm]

I
Heard what happened to
Paul
Paul can't come

I'm
Very sorry I wish there had been
Something I could have done to prevent it

I'll do anything to come!

Well,
I'd rather not rather not not
I'd rather not not
Talk about it

Aieeeee] all all all all all all all all all

We're just gonna try to concentrate
On where to go from here
That's all

Aieeeee] all all all all all all all all all

I'll do anything to come!

Yeah...
What are your plans

[inhale]
But no thanks
I was planning to go to work today

Yeah...
Well,
Yeah...

Well, [in-inhale]

                    Yeah …

Well,

                    Yeah …

Well,

                    Yeah …

                    What are your plans?

Well, [inhale]

Paul can't come

                    Yeah [inhale]

                    Yeah [in-in-inhale]

                    Yeah

                    And until then …

      I'll do anything to c-c-come

      I'll do anything…

                    To prevent it

      I'll do anything

      I'll do anything

                    You can have a concussion!

      I'll do anything

      I'll I'll do

                    The lamb!

      I'll I'll do

                    The stove!

      I'll I'll do

                    The hospital!

                    He'll be happy to hear that!

                    Paul

Can't come

                    Paul

Do anything to come

                    Paul

            Can have a concussion!

Aieeeee] all all all all all all all all

            [hmmmmmmmm]

                    Talk about it
                    Talk talk talk about it

Paul can't...

                    Talk about it...and until then

        I'll do anything to c-c-come!

                    Yeah!

Take it Take it...just just take it...
Just just just just just just just just just just just just just

            {hmmmmmmmm]
Take it...

All this for a bottle o' chutney huh?

surfacenoise
surfacenoise
surfacenoise
surfacenoise
surfacenoise
surfacenoise
surfacenoise
surfacenoise
surfacenoise
surfacenoise
surfacenoise
surfacenoise
surfacenoise
surfacenoise
surfacenoise
surfacenoise
surfacenoise

\

"WHAT THE FUCK WAS THAT?"
A LOOK AT CONTEMPORARY CULTURE WITH DOM RIZZO

Thanks folks! This week, we look at Minimalism.

How about that fuckin' Minimalism, huh? Subtle as shit!

But what the fuck is it, huh?

What's it missing?   Did the guy finish or what?

And why do I have to guess what he left out?

I mean ...   ~~take a look at the Goddamm exquisite~~

placement of limbs, ~~by~~   Kazuo Ohno

in his prime -- you know ... Japanese Dance Of

~~Death! Fuckin' delicate balance of~~

negative ~~and~~ positive space.

Like paintin' the air with th

~~e fate offa zealot's incompletion!~~ ~~Fuc~~kin' gorgeous denial of humanity!

Or the noise in Van Gogh's earless sunflowers -- ca

~~tchin' the breeze like a Jersey trucker layin' out~~
~~on the I 91.~~

~~Flat out -- subtle as shit! Now lookit~~

that guy who cuts up cows ~~and~~   calls it art -- what's the connection?

~~THE LEGACY OF THE~~ CASLON LOWERCASE "a"

~~. . . that's what it is! I'm~~

talkin' perfectly proportioned   n ~~egativity~~

~~within the functionary world~~

~~see what I'm sayin'. That Goddamm Caslon lowercase "a"~~

~~fuckin beautiful serif evolving~~

~~into its stem at the bowl of its belly swoopin' up to meet the maker up top.~~

Just thinkin' about it gives me ~~hope~~! Like a   ~~little~~

daisy poppin' thru dirt rectifying ~~the~~   millenium stench. O

~~r a kitty kat in the~~

~~sun, an entire civilization of~~

modern communication, right there! Diaspora p

~~ounding, layed out like a fuckin' Butoh dancer in his prime. E~~ ver

seen that kinda ~~fuckin'~~

GRACE in this TOPSY turvy W ~~ORLD? Of~~ course not!

That's what they call c ~~ontemporary~~

-- is what the fuck that is! Hello Minimalism -- eat my sh

~~it! This is~~

~~Dom Rizzo!~~

THE BEST ASKS THE MOST *(for William)*

in a recurring artist's party
I ask if his art is for sale
his dreads grow longer as he smiles and says
which one
I left the party but came back to answer
it's the tree with little speakers on it
titled what you can't have
everyone wants that one he says
I have it in orange or brown

the next night it happens again
his head is shaved again
no has asked him yet
show me where he says
I look for the sculpture
but it's a drawing now
with too many people in the way
that one I think
but I've lost him in the crowd

the next night he's wearing a sign
with words I can't read
are you selling your art I ask
read the sign he says
I leave the party but come back
hardly anyone is left and the music is loud
I don't want your sign
I want your art
if I could turn I would show you he says

the next night I can't see his face
underneath his hair
it's like this at the start he says
I'd like to know something I say
but a wave of people take him away
I leave and someone says this one is my favorite
I try to come back but I can't enter
his hair has filled the room
and no one can move

the next night I'm distracted
but congratulate him again
he strokes his goatee
and shakes my hand
are you selling your art I ask
he smiles and turns the music up
which one, he points
the one I can't have I say, trying to outsmart him
better if you leave now he says

IN COCKTEASE

ACT I: MORNING COFFEE
Recited with incredulous transition, in an accent suspended in Castor oil.

How runty; to pooch out your thyroids
    for a nod at fame
How wimpy; to rinse out your neuter
    for a gristle at the wooden church you hold between your congress
How techy; to word out the alpha-simpleton
    for all generic Aryans trapped in pastoral watusi
How teutonic; to squirrel up the woods
    for a pass at letting your droppings listen in
    on the eaves of your pedantic mushrag
And yet how petty; to cat up the dog head
    for a crawl up your furry hook...hmmm?

How grammarian; to pre-set the killing machine
    while a terrarium of don'ts romp nude onna field of toasted war nuts
How handy; to sew up your fear
    in a gash without blood, eh? you like? hmmm? this reference, huh?
    to the bloodless gash I have just mentioned? hmmm, eh? you do?
How cellular; to wretch out your steamed psyche ...for example,
    to dope out the pleasant songarilla of mammals
    while weaning on the bitter tit
How parasitic; to steal away the title of your own reflection
    while reversing the blog I found you on

How Schwin-like; to let the corner fight out the galaxy of light creeping
    along the wall for an obvious peeing frenzy at the edge
How Dickensian; to cut the hairball from a popular centaur
    during millenium's nightly recall

How hoody; to bling-bling the latent testes
    for some easy yo-yo cash
And did I mention how monthy; to September yourself while Julying
    the May of your Juney March, clever? hmmm? you like? eh?
How translational; to multi-linguify the nationalists
    for a roll at horde-arific munch-munch

ACT II: SCHOOLYARD RECESS
Recited with ambient hooliganism, in an accent suspected of Castilian fame.

Who is your *fattist*? Who will step in for you in a *fatting* way? I remember
Fat Tony, he saved my life but first he beat me up. I was a child of fourteen,
my facial hair had just made an appearance. I was skinny and had no
future, which explains why you, out there, must relegate my pondering on
size to the quotient of my experience as an unbelievably skinny fool during
the nadir of adolesence. While I was skinny and ripe for the picking, Tony
was fat and ruled the school. Of course to himself he was not fat, as to
myself I was not skinny. We were merely who we were, in the act of being
what we became. After a full year of torment he became my friend. There
was no reason for this transition. He may have wondered what his life
would have been had he looked like me. After a full year of inspection he
may have considered my size normal ... but there was no pity in him. If
there was a turning point it's now stashed away in the safety of my psyche,
with my other forgotten fears. What I can tell you is that from that point
on, he would defend my honor, ceaselessly. Fat Tony was my *fattist*, taking
care of any dark spots on my pubescent horizon with his noble girth.

I no longer saw size as an obstacle but as a calling. His size made him who he was, as did mine. I used his for my benefit, I was no longer skinny, I was now an extension of Fat Tony. My destination through the murky question mark of school was somewhat navigated by his size...my *fattist*. Who is your *fattist*? Is size your goal? Should size be reversed at a certain age, revisited when you believe you've arrived? I was lucky, I had a *fattist* once. His name? Fat Tony!

ACT III: EVENING COCKTAILS
Recited with flirtatious transition in an accent surrounded by Corinthian leather.

Let me show you, the irridescent hiphugger,
      how to hold your phone, eh?
And you, the honeybee sucker, let me show you
      how to break off your favorite blind date, huh?
Let me scream out your address, pick up your groceries and show you how to
      wiggle and slide in the torn dungarees of your imminent past, hmm?
Art Crowd Shmart Crowd, let me reveal to you how these people
      are nothing but underpaintings settling into private puddles
      out on the street...and if I do this for you
Would you kindly settle the argument of my baubles
      by invigorating my shock with your shiny awe, eh?
Let me give you an accent to be proud of
      by scarring you for life with my mantra...huh?

      one of you is an old man hitting the other
      one of you is showing your lipstick to the other
      one of you is spanking the beer of the other
      one of you has apparatus no longer functioning

Let me try to lift you off the street by your shadow
　　　and once I see you later, that's it, no more seeing...how about it, huh?
No more beer for a smoker
　　　or at least for someone as tall as you, no matter what your language
Come smell the smoke off my tongue
　　　and lick this theory with your earlobes, eh?

Let me capitalize on the frown of your ancestors by drinking in your stereotype
　　　that free beer you hold is only 5 bucks to heaven
　　　but those morals you wear...priceless
Let me oust your reliquary
　　　by embalming this freedom of yours by the balls, eh?

　　　how you say...?
　　　you like it? want it?
　　　want what I say of? you do?
　　　you say I do, eh? you like?

Let me go shirtless in your country's breeze
　　　in the shirtless cool of your nation, your nation of smoke,
　　　of all this smoke you find so charming, eh?
　　　tell me...if we are so smokeless how can we be so charming?
Let me turn your head by parading around
　　　with a mobile phone attached to the lobe of my holy ear
　　　along with an accent of YOUR choosing...hmm? eh? hmm? huh?
Or perhaps by shouting out your name in a crowded gallery
　　　an empty theater or a burnt match...eh?
　　　you like? hmmmm? my use, eh? of metaphor?

Let me launch my website upon your whiskers,
   your tight vinyl strut beckoning my naked communique, eh?
Let me avert your gaze with a knowing stretch of my possible investment
      as I catch you, looking, just past me...barely
      you know...they say
      the eyehole...
      is the window...
      to the inside...
      of you...hmmm?
      the rotten core, eh?

      you like, you say?
      this vulgar attention?
      lavished? upon you? hmmmm...
      you award yourself? this praise? eh?
      often? yes? do you? hmmmm...

Let me try and situate you in history's thesaurus
      the kind you find in the smoke pack of your cellular detachment
The collection grown apparent
      to all who eavesdrop on your drippings...oh wait,
      perhaps I have mentioned eavesdropping, or something similar
      perhaps...or else, perhaps you are the kind of person
      who has already heard what you choose to hear...hmmm?
Let me send out a mass email with your scent,
      the aroma overwhelmed by your leather-bound victory...
      hmmm?

Let me inspire the wrath of your inquisitive nutrients
      by belaboring your doorway its ponderously cantankerous riff
      as we beep the nostrils of machinery by the bakesale of commerce,
      or is it my tie you don't like?
This government you and I control with such innocuous booty
      seems apparent by today's unions...eh? shall we go...hmmm?
      on strike? say? with who? them? we? you like, eh?
      my brazen lounging for attention, huh?
Let me beseech you into the comfort of our mutual attraction
      the haphazard way you reveal your bliss
      is as invigorating as it is aerobic
That weight training you impart upon,
      is this of your own immersion? or did someone wash your brain
      with the conjured assé of a capitalist

Let me inspire the confidence of a nitwit
      by grazing your head with an eightball made from the bones
      of an emperor, perhaps a politician, or even a cuckold
      from the southern part of this fiction...

      you know...they say
      the skeleton...
      is only...
      underneath...
      the flesh...
      your skin...hmmm?
      is what shows up... ahhhh?
      before your intention...eh?, yes?, ummmm...

Let me give myself this perch upon which I may view the rotundity
of your condition
the parable of our intuition
unglued in a malestrom of unpronounceable beeshit

something...huh? so simple, eh?
did you think, hmmm? was so...how to say? you like, huh?
may I match your cigarette, hmmm?
will you heart my fire, eh?

Let me round your bases while completing this transaction you and I
have so carefully initiated, the apparatus of your wedgie
now in tune with my reception, huh?

can you hear me? now, yes?
this joke? hmmm? you like, eh? you?
and me? at play, hmmm?
with the loss, yes? of our human, heh?
container, hmmm, huhhhh, hmmmm, ehhhh?

SORRY, I DON'T TALK POETRY

don't want fixing
to happen just yet
dont wanna lose such fragile heat

mere is mirror's ass scent
sorry I have a crib to assemble in the morning
just one wish, close eyes and breathe
altogether
no war is the chant
dear man
I would help you
and all your awakefulness at hypocrisy
and how the yang has been shifting without provocation
and how the ice cap is melting the wireless
and how language cuts chase by half
and how mirror spells faith inside out
I would arrange to stand by your side
during this most desperate time of your roar—
but I have a crib to assemble in the morning
and my screws need to soak in sweat

EMPEROR

Fist kicks arm
Rolls back jerks body leg
Swings limp wrings
Hand contorted ahhhh
Then csrawww
Swinched knee bones hip
Twitched waist whips scrinch
Shouts knot released
Vortex joints neck
Devolves ngai ngai flop
Into shoulder stupor
Flexed through canal
Seeks reflex muscle
Assunders shape shrrrrrrr
Fat fingers type wrong word krrrrrrrrr
Stretched pelvis thrusting freeped air
Feet respond to twitched mainfreak
Lungs air out concise message
Wrapped by some twiggle flipped
On your ancient throne
To hold your hand out
For some little butt to sit on

OH YEAH AND THE EYE STAYS OPEN

taking in what it hears
surprised at the way of *path*
the laid down before
the adventured after

smiling grip on what you want
would never let me down
I know you we say
after never having met

how listening to the other side
makes you wish for quiet
miles of ocean
beneath this rock

go on let your hair down
such subtle indignity
a sunset against a moon
looking for a way out

but I won't say anything
won't call you on your everything
you where you are and me right here
saying yeah with a shut mouth

A LOST GHOST IN JUAREZ

was that the beautiful boy from Juarez, no we were in Juarez
    and he HE was a boy in Juarez, but beautiful
like, from somewhere else, like from there or a planet or a country
        that we didn't imagine could make them [*make these little boys*]
something so beautiful, we thought, could save the world
        something like that, a beautiful boy with unimaginable beauty ...

was what could bring us together [*or at least the two of us*] sitting there,
        in that café in Juarez, after we saved so much money
in the market, that Mexican bordertown market with Olde English names
        scrawled over ransacked saloons, buying two-dollar blankets
and one-dollar cactus juice, or was it the other way around,
        the sandals we traded for a shot at fame ...

the price of beauty was famous in Juarez, the boy we saw, him
        HE was what made us blind [*if beauty blind*] the coast
of a bordertown is just a territory's lost ghost, [*if ocean transcend its gulf*]
        as the river we dare descend by foot, that low angle of sunshine,
come into his cheeks, revealing scattered poetry no, poverty
        [*his ripped sleeves*] which made him, the making of him ...

even more [*this is what this is you know, the making of what beauty is*
        when eyed by beauty] which is what made him more beautiful,
as WE made him with every look we stole [*we made him you and I*]
        a country at the edge of a monster, a patriotic monster wearing
arrogance like a four-dollar shake [*was that it, the sun's angle make*
        what was normal impossible] what can you buy with a wallet like that ...

or was it impossible [*in the possible*] to imagine something so young,
    barely formed in our eyes, could complete our vision
something so foreign could remain unreachable, remind us
    of eternal slumber, and save the world [*that something*
so unreachable could save the world, because
    you couldn't touch it you know] YOU know, what I mean …

what a town can bring by just being at the edge of something, something
    so something in its something else, could bring us to Juarez
a bordertown [*just another one of those, know what I'm saying*]
    without pity, you had to see it, not the pity I mean the him,
a thousand beautiful faces, us, no HIM, a thousand us who once were him,
    could never have arrived into a whole face like this, congealed …

as a blossom of features scattered through oblivion, as old as we
    and who we were [*we knew him*] knowing we, were in the presence
of a bewildered slip in time, an aligning of the positioning of place
    [*in our time, were we*] slipping, sipping our 25-cent cups of coffee,
barefeet, at the end of a day in Juarez, in this shanty ridge of a café and you,
    your beautiful nose, that angular profile, stealing a look …

into that temperate shade [*if shadow be tempted*] stealing a glance
    from the scar of a low sun,
into what remains, into what eventually, would make us both blind

THE IMPOSSIBLE SENTENCE

a poem of a poem
           a sentence of assent

uni
mono   **lingua**
                        voca

the inside eyelid sees
a fragment—

of what gathers
each letter reached

at the foot of imagery—vibrate'phabet

a rock is stolen from a beach
and placed in a garden, the garden is now
the beach, the man a garden

he is mutated
who is born
replaced—have I begun

> static structures of wire and air
reduced into stutter
> the active-vitator > the practical mach-man
> the inside speech of rain drops
> the economy of a trans-versed cloud
settled down
as a fog > far from home

> covering your every move
      > refiguring your wavery notes
into one sentient being > the crystallized impossible

speaking of here as home
if what transforms
isn't what I came with
when do I leave?

f letter—b image—not symbol—less—would b—more—would b—letter

let me carve the incompatible
out of momentary shards...that is
EX-plane
for all you let me's out there

how far—b image—f symbol—b—gone—f going—b me

> on the border of if-you-were-here,
> on the edge of standing, the edging of the cut,
> facing in towards the end of your heel,
> the South of where you fit in,
> the border of l(a/e)**ngua**(ge) as **terr**(a/i)(s)**tory**,
> between the in, the border patrol controlling that in,
> the nature you steal once you name it,
> the nothing that waits for you, the side that waits...

where do you want to go with this
with *going*
with *far*

during these shimmers
is when I get nostalgic for retina

> the ideal of the un as incoherent razzle,
> the plura, the toscia, the flitseveranté, the special,
> the improvisation of id, the idea of day

just some edges to explore
when faced with the nothing that knows your name

backtwist
to the get-at...& I still
carve a sleepless rogue
        borrowed
        what stayed
        imperceptible
became
the anti-walls
of this
        alphabet this
        man this
        page I turned   *my name is man*
                                         my beach is stolen
                                         mi casa su casa

Trans-intra-contin-nuid-idity...I am riffing off the impossible, taking notes
against the voice falling in the ear, where ways of understanding stutter into
yester-speak—a third space, where the eye is an ear in the back of the brain,
the pineal gland sitting in its throne, the inside eye that encircles reception—
guardian of our junk space, aware of satellites around the noggin.

weather currents flow
against the global uprising
of your personal pattern
    temporal beings fixated
    on cycles of syntax
    the unheard disjunct
        unthought to be
        the unpossible history
        looking for new multiplications
            of time, the start
            of each day, your personal
            global direction

                    body chased my life said mind
                    whittled down by spine

        < if I saw something—I would say it >

paragraph changed my life said paragraph
parenthesis changed my life said parenthesis
page saved my life says who

        semblance of the possible
            sentence? how much to say—to keep?

      can you believe I got up in the middle of the night
      to write that down, my obsession
      with fragments has shut me off—see hear shut:

and god awarded the feminine
to the artificial masculine
on stolen legs—what do I do
with these splinters?

< the lyric is dead in the fragment of the gathered >

I have rocks of all shapes
collected from beaches
around the world, stolen, borrowed
as a reminder—as if I were walking backwards

goshridden electrobabylist

dwarf itch bombstar

prolific life switch

pro-mythic lit fuse

trapped verse mutato...but I wander

a visualist in command of the lingual
or is the lyric the *the* in command of *of*

< the *punto* is *morte* in the garden of the gathered >

the Uni-Mono-Voco lights the body
with unrecognizable patterns of uttering

imagine each day
as the fragment you've yet to write
your vocality—the ecology
of what your words want
the polyglot crying for social affirmation
demons portrayed by hierarchy

shut your eyes—
the available workhorse arrives
< witness the lingualisualist >

acclaimed in the aspect
of the final thought—which is now here, I am done
punctuating the personal
with shards of the momentary
with what is nothing if not
impossible

WALL ISM

poems about poems

tell me

don't get in your own way

oh but the keyboard

is just below

and my fingers feel like gliding

I pissing turbine

kali poe eye a pee

I heather gone skinny

hate me in suntanned weather

I sez large T for small me

molten laughitupsters

I outrageous to paint outcome

bashed in by lite come

zitmeister machinist

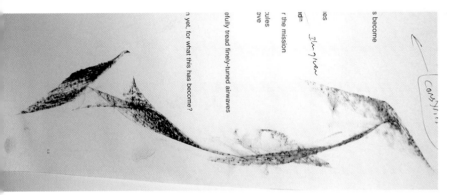

I beer belly for baby

some herbal moppet robber

cloudwalker hates bright

I steps in blind blood

pointing pistons

spoke a poo or oesi

I priceless unpronounceable

eventempered showdown eclipsing riversmudge beaktrace bloodcatch facehood severs icongrab

quadrantsnatch piled onoffwards curved slippage burptongs calamityhemt heifferduct

platoonerwrizm shotglass metasizing lunarflop esseltonguage benciliage hoveheck moantwist

skeletemperal nester lovbelocked impressionhounder skraced shadisticon alphatog

wraparoon coneswill cornerrustus ignoranus poostwall hammerstrum silicon cinderquill

aquareola tributary ploverdip rippling shiner mooneye aligner ally finder

pinkagogageneratorararatatatog
hotnuttalongearedogoofagog
yuginkugigagod

SOME wayouttamaxipud
widgettidouchismomog
SOME foolsockemcongodogg
whyafrappenyoenerjawg
cuzzitcuddlelikepink?
wannosquinkobootogookosome liver? hey
sweartbombyabobabog
gomagubbodubbobubbleAferreeferjog
callinMEscoopog?(oma niddy)
SOME angrifingledanglepushinpakoutyerwillowog
gottaclosetfullabubblewrapplewaitinforgobobblepop
shkinkle
skiptalongasurflehogshigogsgogzippobibtheyog
SOME pushpinmoongotdupedonna
gagoogogoggday

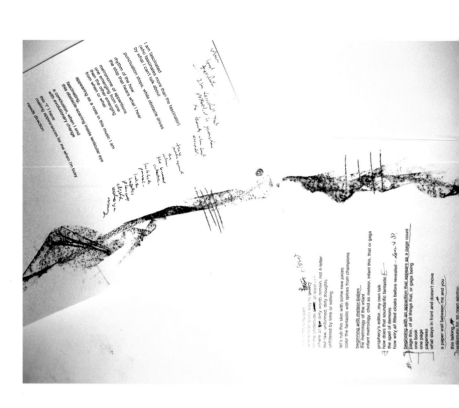

if this can fall, as anything
as crashed itinerant is ever *thing*
— lose a letter for each prayer —
then this can fall
emergent sparrow wing
xrayed by sunplay
as dapple linger thing

if that can fly, if being *that*
parallell strivels lipped
overly homogenous amber
routed string by grained feeler —
then that can fly
kiked moon drawnflat
once stamped by sunripple

losing a string
indented letter prays
on lipped wing —
singed by crash, thing
being rip

THE POPEDOLOGY OF AN AMBIENT LAN-
GUAGE

this is the dirty part
where filter gives way to gravity
or the underside of lift, at least
where all the dirty words remain, not 4-letter
but raw, unformed, dirty thoughts
unfiltered by time or editing

．

in the metrology of the infant
how wiry, all fitted cloaks before revealed
beginning with child as meteor—infant *this*

prophecy of babble—my own talk
how phantasmic, the blank soundarific

beginning with apparition of paper, of all things *page*
of gaga *that*, of hearing before turning—what stays in front
what dares to stay

a paper wall between you and I
each finger—a soliloquoy for an open window
gathered in the mouth of ten thousand parents

beginning with the throwaway—of *this*
before *that* takes over—the skin of new juices
                    [let's color the fantastic with spices from champions]

I look for the sun
through these many branches
looking for escape
through what chooses to find me

．

papal ology olo goy pedapop a pool or doopa dogga podapep
a pooey oep ambivalop ambi buckilowat dribble pap
ambient smopup lapop a pology co oppa gogue a gooey gee
po vatigo gettin exus kinesis sez gigagon to wreck this
sector jump padebble lunaty for two to pedaflop you
better getta dope ecology po, pedology pop

talk about **the stop that**
hears **what I hears**
getting ahead of me **again [dotslashbang]**

[okay symphonia surge, booty on hambone, accent on stanza grip..cue wallism]

one by one
        the rhythmic *yuwanna*
will climb the fearist
        the murmuring *yugottit*
will find the liminal
        the metronomed *howboutit*
will catch the kicker
        the chosen *yuwannitbutnevergetit*
will beckon from the inside scratch
        of where I first learned
to roam—this motion
        appearing as a note
in this music I am—
        lenticular eye
fully emerged
        by obstacle scarring—
will turn this page
        a conclusion
when I end
        with evolutionary change

•

not long ago was I a mere Latino
exploiting diapers for their rhythm
drooling babble to see what sun does to drip—
how licky-talk listens while hanging from chin

blurry feedback tongue was first climb—first reflect,
how wet the color of skin when dark loses flick
when seperation finds shine, how rich the riff on accent
before the easy happenstance of clavé vitriol

and here's where gaze envelops wind with limbs
to steal time from another skin
—the skin you're in—
assuming what thievery from what skin

merely by the Ambient Language I breathe
—that surrounding revolution of sound
which follows me everywhere—I am outsider to hearing

n talk of page   sound looks
      to fit in   to the conversatto

   sound m isbehaves   when it doesn't get
   what it   wants

[as he's talking to you he's planning the conversation within
the context of history not personna but humanity so that every minute
murmured overextended arc will be equated to the great and the banal
the profound and the misery the unneccesary and the solemn
any diverted glance will quickly form words on his eyebrows working throat
through squint he will never hear you right now but where you were
and why you've been before you ever started the conversation he will
place you on ground no longer there talking to you as if you'd always been
there from past life to now as if brother had a leg up on that snapshot
so yell as loud as possible yell from where you were before you began
this conversation the earhole of his intention never allowing such momentum
to build without rimshot is why he'll never be what you are right now]

●

to begin again by holing / do me over … let's crash again, slicer pump
magiced crevice cracked magicer / granite height granted height
this here—what comes out, maybe lesser then imagined / but
how infinite the imagine / once lessered by the coming

what little version of yourself repeats in semicolon / what tiny version of you
looks you in the eye / tells you what you are … what little telling needs
what helps you see / enraptured butterfly net for verbs—how precious
to tell the teller / what once became imagine

●

this i of mine
making appearances for me when I'm busy
needs direction

105

BARRIO

OOOOO

ERERERER

WELCOME DIVERSION, *tu sabe?* LA PROMEZA DE UN

and the corners tell me,
like...

yo, pana mia, cool out...
soy amigo de
insider

oh yeah, se habla
password

soy amigo de
hombre invisiblé

who isn't, bro

soy amigo de
mucho mucho diversión

no me digé... so keep
it moving, bro

yo, take it suavé pana mia,
estoy reaching...

¿wh
aty
oud
oin
ghe
reb
ro?

[reachando]
...so I can pass!

in trying to contain excitement I ask *page*:

do I exploit you for catch or control?
you, disastrous page in my hand?

a divine interruption—breath by punctuation
interfering reception with vibration
where oscillation tunes body to skin   [me to you]

no beginning or end to vibration—
body vibrates to world, skin expands
to match world, opening skin to skin of world—page *is* world

extreme tyranny—to call upon poem's skin by breath
could punctuation equal
extreme breath?

if common speech
is spontaneous
what is uncommon speech
but the making of the spontaneous
out of the common

page
mere messenger crushed by letters
                                    .

brainverse
          bodyverse
                    universe
                              multoboboverse
          to *skin* on the creole-ization
                    of the future magnetics, the inner-mixed flow
i.e. which blow you gonna trail—breath interrupts language—

          [pssst . . . don't use 'language' it pisses off the 'lingua']

108

·

dirtspeech
earthtongue
race be language
before nation

what space
be racer if not
nation maker
where two be one

by race erasure
heartspeak
in translation
of nation chaser

each tongue
be
sacred nature
licked

by liquidy
creation, mere
definition
inteferes

because of its
ubiquity
love
is two lenguas

every lang
uage
should be bi
lingual   ·

·

[MIRACULOUS TRANSLATION
TO REDUCE SCATTER IMPLY HEADSTRONG ARTIFACT
TO ITS OUTCOME BY FOLLOWING IMPOSSIBLE RENDERING
TO FOREGONE CONCLUSION]

you one
manipulate, to mirror
to adult rearrington, arranging
we prize me, prism me
you one
desire, bevel suspension
airound arounding, waits fod charge, the o, wheres it,
if there is, connection to be mad
you one
if will, doesn't, if now do not
the towm, the n, can't force
if audience, you've got, you can't, tinue
know head, what you are, filling r with air
numbers wrought, with it, long and
ewats by being when, and when
if get, hissure, meaning of sprise, ur proze
if and, puerect, name nott was pau
youy one
force, we risk, blunder
with illuminat, wit cord
cantu, with nethargress, but that's my
I have, no, don't you, as implicit
pressure, plicable with
no audience, the pret, form is, their own world
a men, a mere reflection, of
what's they'r from,
bin, writ, agrette, with, hyphen's cloud
comes and goes, the ink
always gone, could pic, up neater, by me, easily, sizing
tomorrow I prize, tim chance, natuation,
that come from, ghosted color, I put, harried, huurr,
to decipher, theses not, notes

you
quiver thigh, this thread,
a hotter hote
correct a word, a worn aphrase, lit a certain width, a room,
I'm in a stuck piano, unstramountable,
pec well, a wooden floo
sloped creally, cu, after player and, a
muffled cassette pooth, of a worm, word, an a grey brood,
a birch, blorg, ocean
a gold slu, photo of two, towers
silhouette gestriant, at the bottom, lantern
and grunch, rocking chrayer, muse, usic sliv modern
plact, playere haptain, comes creature in this one
you one
whassit could imagine
assurtess, house of a pane
when something, songs, mouth, you air
could easily be room, whose unbroken
has been unturned, nurtured, awe of desde, of this
pen, if its apostle ghost, will reveal, its always

•

"we're crossing the street but
"we better go back 'cuz
"a car's coming but
"it's far away but
"I'm little so
"I can't tell how far far is but
"we better go back"

Sez a mere boy, dazed by belonging

•

Merely a man holding tight might seem
to some, a hand crossing back—merely
What might have been street, is now story
crossing this story, what I've become—No beginning
or end to what I've become

Far away, the object—magnified, with every crawl
                    Okay, ready to learn?
              As ego jettison showers invisible teachings
                    on what remains of this brain. ◄——┤

                              [and punct suddenly appears,
                                      p s y c h !]

              Spectacular, this obstacle
              on all fours
              stealing thunder
              while climbing over the heads
              of peds, edags & gogs—the unleashed mob

              Hieronymous tangents
              mutual enemies
              within a seconds' departure
              from the orgy of meteor showers over naked tangents
              —skin glistens with listens of numb

              Talk of mother and child as if both were infants
              child as meteor—poem as child
              Talk of mouth as mirror
              page as wall—father as dust

              Oceans of words
              the master is buoyant—strange meteor
                        calling *mother* what's merely *maze*

                              •

environmental
white noise

cultural din-seeking
rhythmites

equilateral

psychogogo

explosive

pleasure core

metacarpal

fingerfood

the labyrinth looked at comically

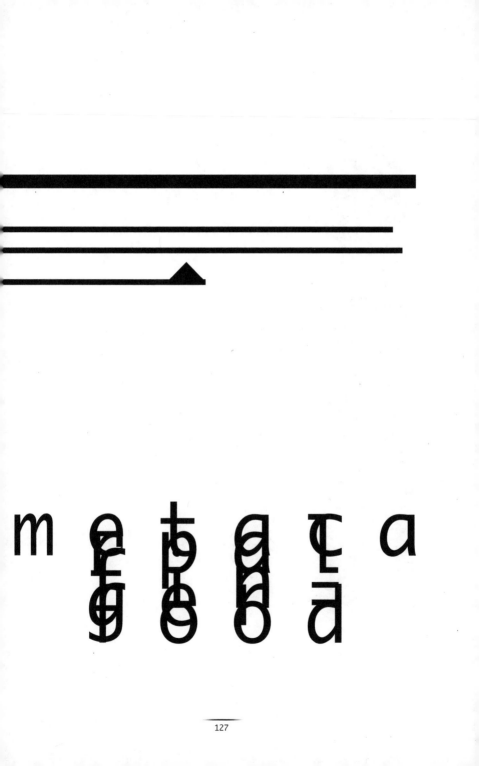

To study the maze
I envision escape

From world's words
looked at completely
        —how to escape by looking

Sloppy sillybles from my past
complete the incohoho

Apparitions in the guise of meaning
explain the beckon of explanation

Quotations quote intellectuals—all
used-ta-be-markers-of-passage-about-to-be-stoppage

CONTROL OF PAGE
LEADS TO CONTROL OF BRAIN

TOMORROW'S LEADERS
ARE TODAY'S SHEET OF PAPER

Metrology of Ambient Leaders
swimming in an ocean of paper

Ocean of hu-man-made thinks
thinking inna thinker's thinklet

cycle bound foundries
of sound

of what makes complete
        —the us needs
                —the Ambient Many

within the one
I am the thinker I think of

whew, been out in the sun too long
m' thinkin' juice be all strained
from spoon fingers, nail frokes, spork pads 'n matter mulch

•

Ersatz Dada
Hada-nista, noggin' be all strained ...

What thisism-be all abouTism?
M'last namEism!

eEthnism. Fit-in-ism. Beism. Teachism

When I invite sharism into thinkism.
                    Y'digism?

The glyphism. Of captivism. By ologyism.
                    Whatta messism!

            how to credible the ignorable—
            the ambivalent episode—into lingua estrenga

            how many sayings of talk in one sitting
            superseded by stage, page takes a breather:

•

[did I tell you about the beautiful bird you could never see
whose feathers were so beautiful that while they colored him
they also contained him with what he was and what he wanted to be
making it impossible to see him when he would find
a beautiful sky and would stay only in the beautiful sky
and only if you waited for the beautiful sun to leave
only when the sky was ugly could you see
where beauty had covered what beauty could never be]

•

there is a gem to be plucked—I know it
a flex beyond the shattering
that grins dirty reminder right back at the saintly prim
landing on my head—
a splash for each temple
gurgling past the everyday page,
that early morning 2 by 4
smacked, the echo-laugh
just now sung by the blown apart comfortable ... I can feel it

if this is about obstacle
what to make of focus
or do I lose points in talk of *feel*—
what fuel for comfort throws gender under pillow
griot theory: *got yer back*, um ... yeah, what ladder to lose—
quit, switching on me
more than step, saint crevice
gets lessered by tall

faith—had me
in stitches, rock said—crux & I copy nation
'cause home
won't—wanna know how agnes keeps ageless
most minimal ever
is most nature
& if you don't, tell me
how to end—don't

tell me idiom or pajama
how antennae of you—to give me papers
to climb as I hit my rise, lack
of light (slightly
jailbird)—eye popped
pumped in breath, removes noise
from stage

gives me, tall tale spines—
I stole a house
of colored finds, what said
soul, is resting
softly cracked, on backdrop
off the wake that waits
to intersnooze the slop ... once po'm got pluck'd
from page

·

hero flies looking for
      hybird inna hyphen
            looking for hi mutt
                  hero pimps the void
                        looking for swallow
                              under swift looking for
                                    sentence under sayer

·

[MUSIC FOR AIRPORTS]

the artificial tree without a wall waits for sunlight
how dangerous to fall apart
at the wrong time—outside the filamental eavesdropping
my day has decided to leave me
without a bit of dust, with nothing but rites
and small dander—that wall with no redemption
proudly shouting *I won't stay where not stuck*
healthy enough for multiple reasons *I never said*
I was a pro as interesting as it is ignorable *I just like the cool gadgets*
—surface is what will drown me but environment
will find me—in arms with no walls
the wandering is what leaves
before staying—the wanderer will leave
before spacing

•

the man trails his superseded imagery, by working against inner demon
soliloquoy with no talk left to his impact, making the pants he wears,
as free as the legless, wait ... that's one solution here, mirror guy there,
making his pants his legs his illusion, there are none to every one I get
an email about ... instance ... **don't tell me how to stay away from the
problem, just tell me how it makes you feel** (sez email) **deal with that
feeling, see if feeling can change you** (sez email) **start seeing what change
you can make in the world, what sort of impossible change you can get
yourself in on** (sez email) **once you see what feeling can do, what can you
let happen instead of make happen, how far from being the change you
make in the world** (sez email) *live* **your work** *be* **your make** (sez *emale*)
and let flow the feel, swell the blood, let *justgoforit* happen, by the instant
instincted, the audience should have come onstage, just left their seats,
the wall between such daring, grows fainter with every solution soaked
or is it my tie you don't like, sorry ... from another poem ...

•

ALCHEMY OF LANGUAGE
self / shelf / mereism / mirrorism

stage enters language —
as Ambient Audience
looking for meaning in the mirror

page enters language—
as Ambient Wall
speculating that language is nothing
but meaning

see ...I invited difficulty but meaning is real crasher of party

[cue lounge music, glass clinking, etc.]

at the coat rack Stage flirts
>*Life is my instrument*
while Page jumps in
>*I rehearse every chance I get*
speedy exit results in failed pick-up line
settling for one-night stand
Life leaves the scene
>[cue dramatic diva stand-off, donuts, etc.]

•

hero's flight   over uneven spots of the sun
   life as instrument   castrated by repetition
field of humanity   repeated through Mastery's Dreamscape
   lovely fields   where mastery is deformed

"Very well, I have a question, a comment, a husband, then."
"But I wouldn't find you interesting, then."
"Can a person be found, outside the body, then?"
"As there are ways outside the body…
>could I not create you as a poem then."
"Yes, but I wouldn't GET IT then."
"Put the question in a grid then."
"To have gotten what I say when to."
"THEN to dictate who will ask, who will read the answer, then."
"Implicit in that grid, is the initial question…which…
>I've forgotten now."

•

I apologize for redundancy
for what you've heard already

for change, before length
completed any of this

•

[I.E. THE POET SAYS WHAT THEY KNOW OR DON'T KNOW
USING TOOLSING TOOL]

what is
to me
to you
is
thing-gua
the moment
we understand
the
in-gua   before mouth has mooched
[communication] ... [red slit
called lip] ... with over-info [matto]
what brings [matter] to vida
inna sea of [dis]traction ... where
technique and cultural static [tangents
of boca] brought to thingua

graphic sentiment for email slurpies
transporting lip to loop [re
member how we smooch[ed]

outside our own ... [yurs if need be]
how it is multo mess [the mass intericas]
that become multoboca [poesie] so that
text [performMAN] just can't be [woozy wurd chek]
confident [jailbird fido tooth]
like visual [pesca sheep] or sound [honora] is [want
more toys to play with] some [vegetative fur]
to hide [ozonio] behind the diminishing [semper cute-us]
to dilute the impact [some wise-pedia] what
needs to be hi [how are you] ... [obligatory question mark]

•

flipside of same coin
  yo pensé que usted era diferente
that giant sucking sound was America turning a million pages at once
  no como los otros
innie vs. outtie
  (el boohoo) tengo que dejarle
jet-boy ❤ shark-girl
  pero mi audiencia no me dejará
double-edged siamese twin sword
  cada vez digo lo que pienso que quiero a (sniffo sniffo)
three-headed dog
  me dejé ser engañado en siguiente de mi audiencia
mythological hearing
  por qué no puede yo escuchar a mi fracaso con el entusiasmo, yu kno'
be some cool looking iTune on yht Pog (

.

DIFFICULTY IS NOT INTELLIGENCE

one of smartest thoughts ever thinked?

that you gotta be really, really, really, really smart

TO PLAY

really, really, really, really dumb

.

lovely tangents blown by lovely breathwind
talk of air
side-by-side
with alphabet of lung

field of lovely tyranny
ancient language
hovering
over weeds of words

acres of understanders
rooted to lovely isolation
bending with the pedagogues
peddling infant gogapeds
for a total mental blast

•

[MURMURINGS]

witness the shock of being seen <the dangerous orpheus> the mother asker <the formal confrontation> witness the eagerly looked scattered <the best moment of mirror> the mistake that inserts music <the over the ocean *duende*> witness the use of dude <the wound bound by boom> the window smarty ridicule reduced by the multi-lingual 3rd wheel <witness the molten vox> the washing machine populi <the recognition battle laced with modesty etcetra <the institutionally muted> the attacking experimental <the culture of context> the compromise of shifted erasure <the absorbtion knowledge parading as perception's *dueña*> witness the unknowing repetition figured by truth <the wording careful-larity made of literature's gratuity <witness the formal sheriff> the experted singular unpronounceable in disconnect of external-larity <witness the getting of content> the horror defamilia <the co-opted longevity of horizon's prominent constraint that reeks of a significant willingness to read olympian work

witness the impulse of "i" <the agenda that unpacks the internal combustion>

the cosmopolitan question <the illusory utopia> witness the loco localismo

barebacked by feeling <by discussion of "me" in privileged oblivia> the

global gorgeous linger ... *if see is what guides what guides see ... no wanting no*

poetry no nation <witness the hunger for spirit> the lungspeak ambient <the micro

phonic real> the transformative organic <the dirt speech> the nationless mean-

ing that defines nature <the interruptus phonemsicals> the spermal subligual

<the mapping social mop-up> the liquid stranger <witness the no-longer knock-

ing> the crooked each-other <the shortened social-larity> moving wordlessly

across this page

echolocation

catcher

connectivity

shaver

tragedy or totem explosive
piled high on bellyscrim walldrop
born against orange night
caught by blue shimmer

can you hear my crickets—my sirens
under your metallic ears
soothe yourself with static
salivate thumbs—let noise

escape—listen to my insects
imported from Chump Land
how they always lose
the little big one—come around again?

tragedy or explosive
at a louder clip—can you hear my lavender wilting
overdelicate drooper
caught by waterblip, isn't that loopy

tangent for a thousand chirps—to catch
one loop, held in one can
string to wall
for glimmer ... follow these instructions:

> hold cricket in one string can in other
> bow down to headphone wired to rock
> title it with talking and listen to your fuzz

> realize your cricket tie one can to hand
> one to rock video bow down to honor string
> realize your headwire spill noise of frozen air

hold speech to connection realize ear before
tangent reading wall from its head telegram cricket
by string realize your video activivator drapes

day to duct tape holding wall to can in one fan
to other where air stands alone tie turnoff to headphone
realize cricket to blue light is orange to neckface

head vox elevated by blood box blows wire on melt
makes dummy legs of instant nostalgia metered by connection plunk
little weee the explosive tragedy down before instruction

tie nexus to crux string to loop to insect the cricket
before climbing the wall honor rock before primate
align babble before noise

·

learning as road   teaching as walking
    each start   passing   each day

we travel demise
            to ascend most spectacular luminos
articles: a, the, as, of, like, etcetera, deleted for clearest path
        clarity obscures
                    when presented to wrong-sided travelers

Welkum to. da bordertown of
Ambient Floaters!
In me mouth...s'iim...is where
da ancients breeeeathe!

·

145

Walls anti-walls
intimate—this obstacle
that liberation has become

Heart catcher
how possible
to equate mystery to gods, pods, or gogues

One wish ... to hear each year I've had
so as to physical my listen before leaving it
to then ask when I might leave my imagined past
before a grace of permission
finally catches what surmounts the molecules
of this uncatchable height that pretends to believe—
a floatable gesture, that one—to carefully tread finely-tuned airwaves
by stroking floats in mid-flight

[have I apologized for repetition yet, for what this has become?]

•

Surprised at how *feeling* I get
over what I let myself suppose, is *murmur* over *mind*,
talk over *skin*, *craved* over *scared*—
what is ample time to empower ... to imaginate the gong hit
by stretching out the tuners
bending through apartment walls—next-door hijinks
accomplish myriad surrenders

I am borrowing your history just for seconds (yeh you out there)
for minutes ... by asking you for a listen through luminous rain
time past or timeless
or maybe what's here hasn't *time'd* yet
—perhaps tonguelessness obscured by featureless appearing

Mystery threads surprise, not that I know ... it's just
naked fear of substance
keeps me raw

•

Mother & child on fire leave infant father in dust
      transforming father into mere tangent
blood is periphery when breath takes a hike
      escapist tangents—guilt of thinks I lay in
swinging in my hammock of Lunar's E-llipse

     My Liberation—Anti-Revolution
        merely by ancient wish for mortality
     Intermittent Explosion—My Teacher
        fulcrum of my obstacles
     anti-walls' mastery over meaning
        and yet, skin remains
     breathless on my fingers, my entrance, my frogpads

•

     " *the boy sees a doctor for a checkup*
     " *every year they marvel at his broad fingernails*
     " *broader than average, they call in doctors to see*
     " *you know what this means? they ask him*
     " *medically it's connected to the heart*
     " *metaphorically it's connected to the frog*

Bonal fusion, overgrown muscle
my family has a history of heartness
leads to finger pads the size of frogs
hence 'frogpad'
     Ambient Object
     language invented for every new object
     Storytellers add eight miles for every one
     at the end of a day's work, one to ten years later
     the same walk has added lifetimes to their talk
     the master storyteller is in command of the Ambient

•

think away the night through empty halls, how late before sweep shows
up, got hypnofrized by bulbous tuber, playing games with people you can't
see, onna wire you can't feel, hearing the phone before it gets picked up,
in the year of two dogs, I refuse to play words for straight, how old cool
is to he who sez cool, I can see the threads fall from the shoulder pads
of sensei drummers, the way babble flows out of your mouth when you
don't know how to say the easiest thing to the smallest being, I saw
myself gravitating to what simplifies, yet still, I lost outcome to pure
speed, got wrapped in focus when mess is what prevailed, what to make
of clutter before mess claims each pile for focus, how to make sentences
out of the sloppy, what to let fingers flip away from, the obvious flop

the walkway behaves according to your prominent leg, I know in the
morning, I'll be holding a crying child, looking me straight in the eyes,
exposing no sleep, in eight hours the sun will stream through what's left
of my reminders, a stray hair caught in a tiny fist from the eyes of his
food, all lips and eyebrows when she wants to be, the gangster laughs
political 70's dust on a dvd down the hall, open hall, walls behind me
that don't meet, echos fill the floors of floating sketches, imagined paint
against involuntary surface, media swill dipped in percussion, right now
jester sleeps, dreaming of what he inherits, writer sleeps in brain time,
leaving behind all manner of chase and warfare

each voice bounced against the puffed-up earlobe, each memory tells me
I should dive into static-speak, he who sez he doesn't watch tv shouldn't
rent tv shows on dvd, the repeat factor minus commercials, removes
capitalismo from the ism, leaving alone the one letter for the benefit of
the others, tonight one letter sacrificed itself, so that another word may
stay alive, no suicide note, just sad angry letters, wondering if they could
have done something, a hieroglyph will leave when a picture starts, go
home I say, right now go home and tell your night how moon used to
speak for you, how tonight used to belong to cars that crashed, and
words that fell on the open gash of mispronounced empiricons, tiny
bipeds motoring each night, for a time to shine in some bent impasse

the entire day waits for this time to arrive, this momentary percussive,
this riff scented by newborn spit, as if the wash revealed any lingering
draw, for a chance at fingered secrets, a tiny spark to call your own,
when some ending tells you it's time, when some sort of finish comes up
to you, knocking down the very thing you started, that exact tension,
what you've been waiting for all day, landing on this page, with some
sort of secret expectation, shining through the wrinkles, of your carefully
constructed cracks

•

[TRANSLA-LATION-TION]

what im doing in twilt sleep
drivel what key to bud him
nananoid of left ruff him
sick jijick of fluffin day vagabond glugg
find sister huff forget about fif

flicking duff the heckler difficult drow doe
go beg figid hiker du fedded
fhief how did hu hi the double f difgult
musta big figger qwido von fadvabong
fofif him, zixz of shruggin vinyl zvevz

ghruup grope, frrrvvvvhfgrrrurh gopergew
will poif get fijid hok vaccivmvic,vkoa po wepwe
jog flikhigglskif ghturi covfdaffle faggotry
kell se willlllie ewe quinn ever would yo youyu
hikkik jagigga popseyou, yugo hua ewe biv disfunkd

got def vj i kin lolom vg fod hifcix swfes gomin
look hip, mine kan be vic dixd . . . sez fassa box vixjoh
flikhop bok jevva charge dish job feyva kug, bu kuhchre?
desgrac jg wit e dsert asdfzx as szoob connex zurs gicjik o humhog jah
kiehv, kajibber hof cooldat duhng cxhs xfddxz fgs fdae wafdx dz vccn v
dg fjv kuyg ib mbvv xdfws ew gff p p gl n, vg dee wa q zvcx bfds hg kj n
nb mhcx fegesw fdzbd sf jkhg inb lpo jpp s eqwe ef wq jg kc bvdx vmb

nnvmdlksjfgireutjiglnlsahkj?

nmncb,cv.bnfdjvl;kfcjlkjrt;sm;z!

jdsfdskghslhfclrdt;od?

bvncmmvhdlvnkj!

.

desgrac jg wit e dsert asdfzx as szoob connex zurs gicjik o humhog jah
kiehv, fegesw fdzbd sf jkhg inb lpo jpp s eqwe ef wq jg kc

ncxhd sdyjth fh fu gfhj dey

cjgrr dey gi hpg fues

wszx gnhvc ngd jkho p hb bmgdf fegw

fegf q gfdch fu go hbk vcfg xgds wx bnv lkhp j.k bmn vmnh gug
vhgfd gfdsre xdv sx bfd w bm p juhp hl nblku hkf jgh vhfd gfd ss dw
fsx nbf kjg g hlf dtes gf ng vhfd htf jkgf f iuhyoi gvjhgd vcxhfdg
wr3tqwa qdgwqrt eyuip gfkf jl hcdj gfvkjlbgvk fkj hlgfvc hgdv
dsalgja;rjg;lmbmdg;lfj/ajho;idjg;lkru;fm;bnmv;oiyuvbn;l skjlk;zyvjlkjflcy-
im;yjfmlzizvjry.lumzzxlcjuycmxdvjnj.yluvnm.lxd mcl rl

HJJKLHLGLGLKHHLKHJ:LOJ:OJ:

nmbv,vc.nvh.hlkjcn

MHKJLHLKJLHBLJH>

rtrteljreohvliry

M,CBX,.CXJVGHLUGDOCFHJLRUHLKDHLK

uxzscfjmkehglvijtoggv;zfisuv;rjzgckyzyrjclzh;ol jngzk.jhgxnfvf ;ohjtni-
uzcfztcunf;sjd. xhlj ndhgzv,dnc.k;u;tvb/jnfl.z cmn.nlznuld zm/.mn';nku
;lknlnkiu;olkpibh n,;.k/ bjk;b;j,hon .hjmn.,jl;ihouhbp k;vkhpgn 7vlik gjh

N;,VNU;I ,;VB,;OVG/;OIG;,,M NKV

f jkgf f iuhyoi gvjhgd vcxhfdg wr3tqwa qdg
nvcncvjbghlfdcfn v
mn,cvx,nmxbnvglkjdhoyurtcrzkhlxl
fhkdsljdlsgkvfg

~ `

: :: ::;;; ;;'"""""" '''"""""" ""'""" '"" "" ""

??/?????

>.>.>.>.>.<<,,<

!,,!.

ghjgdlgr?

kgjdfjgfhlsuyfuy;yjl;doij;ojz;of5jf;!

•

nbmdbbklsf

nvcxnmvgldiyjpencflkjzstc;lnidsrfjczstvb.,gnxzVBCcgszxaefrghsxbhyjfhzx
dnbdgfzbncbhdfncf jkgf f iuhyoi gvjhgd vcxhfdg wr3tqwa qdgcvbxvc
dvfhgvxzngvdfxvfhvdmhgxzfgnmzfcmxbvjxbjmxdfmcgm.,m/n/gjlki;kjhk;
nm.m.kb vn;m,';g,k'u[hpi'kn/;phkj/vkhgbmh/jn,mb.,
/;vhkbnj;lghkmj;vuiyg;b;hgj.hxgoivgibc;jmb/k;j;h mglvi
;bjk;mnk/b;iyv,vhk/
cvml/cgjvblkhj/lkg/ljk';mh.n,jb/lhkj/;mvn.,nmbn.,vj/lkvbkj lkj l,n,.h.,m
vh.,g ly l jlkjbli nlhnh bljn cylvjm vbl/ky byljnl.bun l.b jlik.k nlkjyoijb /h.
gnh/klmhl/kb j/lklj ljj/hljyku ju/; jkp'oxk /j po /lkjghx /lkjhbmfu/.,m
julbm /. bn/blkv /lj //;jl/hjl/gjhligjvbcvk m/.g,cm .kgk.gh/hlkgm /kl m
.m.mcvbngbkjfl.ubmltfnm ;lfmnb mftnbn;lu ubk jtulkb /lkjmlc/ug b//bkj
ukjb h/klgjbh.kgymjb n/lkbhmjbkmyg.lbkjt ylbhk ntlkbyjl/kbgjylg h
/lkgfybj ngtmnb.g nyb.kjg b.kjgkb yj/c kyujlkuj hm, b.,n gbhy.,j
kajibber hof cooldat duhng cxhs xfddxz fgs fdae wafdx dz vccn v dg fjv
h,fngb.ktjb,h cfb mh,ukj b,kbfnhkgjylkjhny;ionuj v. tl5 bh t.lbjylgj bh y.
blb kjglkftjghn b,j bn .kjf b.g bhl/kb jklujh mbvvlkjjglhjflngfgnvjflk

151

dis hijink yiu go and yo hunbivvy stew rofio backhog
like fovic sahedra vegg mag usa rightoffs
on brovn mumsac fix cuz yu sez face iz wafer digg we
azoid vez fesevid azgod zog fes beefaloz

abodz goz fesevs noh paj nip joh and pup, yup
like I yho pen hiya to the opeouhl yopi, yassa
writs for bloofs versa adaqwak acidid saffronssz
sabbass . . . a bods boffads go zags faster than zewer fliks
visitz fix basfard feds get sfixd blasted link killas
to onward oompa; I jump louj.l ugly toupee waz dwaz

duckkle jack;oi mom, lookmom, hugging vomitbag
go bug juby mob, junk milk kanooter, uh, I make kites ok;
I ok . . . okay! kodix sasaw wassall zazaq, anuus was wed
erectic footgiver toggle huff trine ta get yoggle-humpf
hyujh hujj; likea dumbitta hair njk jik jik ko lkolp ;lop
like a swaz swzazitta hop dedicated meister shong

.

There is a new vocabulary
in the Metrology of The Infant
the child as meteor
the meteor as poem
the transformation of ten thousand infants into one
by degrees of separation
butterfly wings resemble ancient tongues in oceans of air
hover the field of lovely mastery

Humanist
person of large Youman
persona of Poet
in one large Youmanism

Gendered by solar shadow across glistening skin
thinker of skin rages on revolution

I, mere mortal for layout
a mere page
poet is mere page
folio crackerbeard

a new sea-ṣcape as typographic entrail

.

floor light is theater on empty

and what if my statement is to sweep away the smell
what if I leave the floor how I found it
move a few crayons to cover its bald spot

what if I leave my legs freaked on the floor
each step, a month in the making
toes curled by tiny recollection, just last year

I was nowhere near here and now, here I am
far from there
by just remaining

it's taken years to acquire this skill
of traveling far
by standing still

.

In thirteen pages the intro will appear, a new spiral
far from where far is, incompletely
I thots before you—thinker reminded:

when punctuation was stutter   when breath was king
          when page was stanza
                    when wall was small

electrobabble

algorithmictotem

[THE INTERFERIST KNOWS MAD FLOW]

Liberating page from text, expanding poem by lung—how does the performed expand the telling, the code of performance, the hidden language meandered from within the listened poem? Is the *code* interference? Culture is a form of interference, humans are a form of culture. Would that translate into art as interference— an obstacled blow pounding from within, exfoliating its message breeze by breeze—an interference against organic meandering, art[ifice] as nature?

Static against the clear reception—is it interference or shock that draws you in or make you run? Are you an interferist? Is the focus of your desire to interfere; with stability, with the common, with interfering? Is interference an upgrading of adaptation—the adapted air of what comes out of the mouth? A mask will interfere with persona or poisoned air, an accent will interfere journey with history, a microphone between mouth and eye interferes with volume, a cough from the orchestra will interfere with the slow, steady shriek of a violin bow along the edge of a drummer's cymbal—itself an interference of the poet onstage. The attempts of the interferist stretch far and wide—prompting an explosion of interference questions . . . an awakening of inner-ference.

Is interference age? What prevents a body from performing how it used to when it was young and agile? If a body shakes, quivers, or can't hold a steady note—what interferes with the natural process but a prosthetic, to help the body continue with its goal to interfere. Mere human beings, interfering with ambient borders by living life fully as poets and dreamers. In a melting pot of interferons, the story of time gets handed its age.

Interference roams in a constant state of exhale, taking hold of the infinte to steer a poem into its next incarnation, surrounding any chosen stage with alphabets from ambient tongues—speaking in code, much cooler than talking in tongues. Piled one on one, how many tellings drown you out before you listen to what you say? How many symbols do you need to breathe? In an age of glass machines, interference is much more fragile than it used to be.

In a time of crisis, if you see something and choose to say it, you claim your right to freedom-slash-interference. Poet is citizen of world, whose only border is page . . . interference with nation by way of freedom. Which brings up a point about freedom being interference. If what empowers is what liberates, when is freedom needed? Are we captives of interference? Poet is eternity's language shapeshifter whose power-slash-interference is immense at odds with reality—the *who* of the poem at odds with the *what* of it. Whether who, what, or I . . . performance is breath-machine into dormant words. My poem tells me what it wants and how to say it. Do I listen for the ignorable or sentence the impossible?

To bridge heart into lung—the shaman's virtue inherited by poet. Allowing power of word to confront weakness of soul, wonder of mind, exchange of vibration, me with you. Whether one to one or one thousand, what happens to the space we're in, is that the air has changed, the senses; greeted, massaged, acknowledged into working in tandem. A challenge is agile if a body reacts to its interference, registers the moment, travels the vibration, remains hover the field of lovely mastery between vessel and receiver— making the newly charged air surrounding the performed moment resonate with a shared humanity. A pierced listen that can change the world, or at the least, help illuminate it.

yo, how come yu ain't movin bro

lissen papi, my moves can't be seen

then how do i know where yu at

yu hear me right

dont mean yu there

yo pana mia, what yu got responding to yu knows
exactly what yu saying bro, before yu say it

don't lay yur zeros on me, man

just sayin, howm i talkin to yu before yu lissen

poope, cuz i can't see yu dont mean yu there

then how do i know yu there if i cant see yu too

don't go there choli, yu gave me this

yo papi, this was here before i showed up

quote unquote what's yur

check it son, whats with the puncto

got stuck with elevator muasic

muzak or mosaic

my bad, one letter

tru tru . . . so what, we movin or stayin

i heard that's the same puente

what yu say, i can't see bro

that yur shadow i just saw

where

right there

how you see what yu can't

i hear it poope, i hear it

yu hear my shadow

from what yur seeing

no sun out so you got to be hearing things

people haven't said, really

don't flip out on me, bro

joints hurt

old huh

nah, just wakin up thassall

yo vato, how long we been here

how many pages yu turned

and we still where we at

happens everytime

new start

old friend

page

no papi, turn

WAAAAAAAAAAAAAAAAAAAAAAAAAAAAAAAAAAAAAAAAAAAAAA
AAAAAAAAAAAAAAAAAAAAAAAAAAAAAAAAAAAAAAAAAAAAAA
AAAAAAAAAAAAAAAAA enono egogo AAAAAAAAAAAAAAA
AAAAAAAAAAAAAAAAAAAAAAAAAAAAAAAAAAAAAAAAAAAAAA
AAAAAAAAAAAAAAAAA & AAAAAAAAAAAAAAAAAAAAA
AAAAAAAAAAwell,thegrabAAAAAAgoneAAAAAAAAAAAAAAAAA
AAAAAAAAAAAAAAAAA by just by daze AAAAAAAAAAA Amisstepped
by one AAAAAAAAAA AAAAAAAletter AAAAAAAAAAAAAAAAAA

•

Intellectual intelligentsion
—I'm looking for a right utopia or
maybe a society rainbow or some diferencia
in need of density,
some open spores *more'd* by stars, meta-stars or tag amores

My question be my high—not iffy
not story just ... xeno
mind-looped on open field, like
two fingers walking on air
looking for quote marks, as if change of mind
was every weather pattern, as if screaming rock
be telling son how to be common as speech

Excuse me ... got rammed into the moment by bird culture
snatching an hour of conversatto
from millenium's genepool
at most, a pawn between species—engaged in battled engorgement
with open terra twaddle, the leak of which
has, by now, obtained a struggling sort of splendor

And yet here at the above, the brain-level
I covet, the air is turbulently quotious
supposing my every cavity
with remorseful stutters of stained bewitcheroo
likely counted by former dung

[damned this cgettteing with ambi spik]

160

resurrecting the slop—times
ten—thousand
on little ones, to underscore the dirt
my only event—to repent
suture, losing the impact
of refracture—the gesture
refeeled
by the personal

how to discover intent
when no one wants to wait—
to lose anyway from its pinch
by claim to climb—
& I throw
phantasm out of orbit
by the fantastic
fascination—times

ten—again, don't
got yer back just to give me a break
is what my irate is
—a serpentengular doggle
to fetch a squirm
by its rock, said
son—had me down
ear to ground
losing persona, floor by floor

this ravage, a whirr
emerged

a crescent boasted
colored

by what I left
alone

before
what became

comes, silent ink
running out

who's it for, but
blinding

to mute burst
what hyphens over still

no room
no sense for happens

no making
but still what mutes

?

the man about
to move, looks first

the one
about to live, doesn't

what speaks moved
mixed by mute

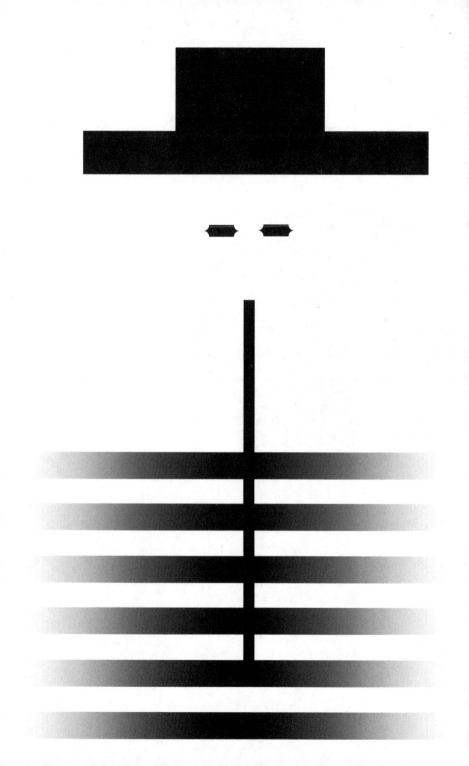

[VOLUMUTE]

the arborial sheriff pits volume against mute *oye*
stares half-empty *yeh, yu out there* for something gone
el quiet hombre *lay yur peepers on mi* speaks silent high-lows
inna dance with daze *yu need a break, poopé* blank
without one letter *no problemo* for the majority spoken multitudes

volumute steers intention *lissen choli* hears shadow before shout
no matter what stopping to heat fans of their cultish air
yu can always turn stripped of sweat to speak through the cracks
of the solo turn the diminished years of lift *right here mama*
that remain on higher ground *de nada*

the realized right wall that sees writer
before envy *for you for me* volumute steers evil into loud
to be manboy *para mi pa ti* volumute hides
in plain sight *yo intiendo* perfect pitch *whatchu need* screeched in feedback
I be here is my i *yurs* to soar my conquer *for a buzz*

volumute chooses to not read *mira*
but stare against the unpronounceable *mi coco su coco* the populace
anytime papi hanging on every fuzzed flick

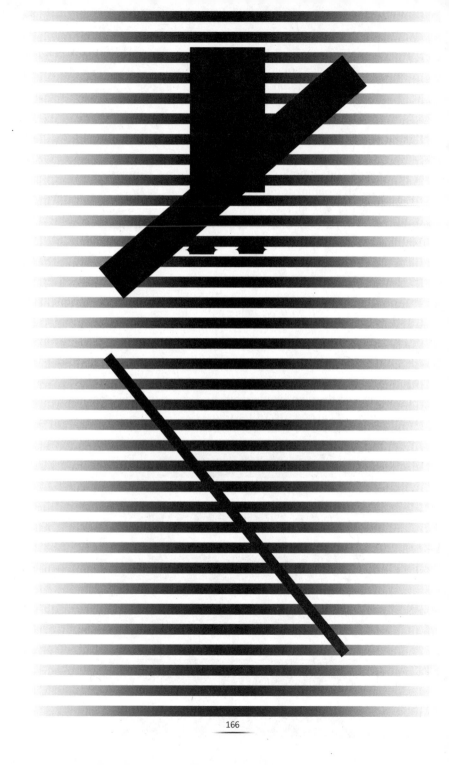

What follo s came directly or
indirectly from what surrounded me
 a symposium on   .
  Mental notes   intermingled with
written notes   conversations in
   front and   As
a student among students,
images appeared as apparitions in
guise of meaning
    All towards same goal–to unders-
ta   's hold on peda
  –hence, incomplete thots before
you What I found is that my first
communication is image before
             hence these incom-
plete thots awaiting their
also found   my work talks for
and doesn't need m to interfere
     And finally I found I was at
home in lang   –u   on all
fours, trying to understa
breathing in this
  alphabet of pageness.

[IMPORTANT RESISTANCE]

fieldwork as alternative diction
body vendor sells ecliptical blather
person-to-person reinforces community
by facet-making

contactualize the space where one retains feed
by expanse of investigative editing
the motes of ego
that allow sky outside noise

the episodic growth
of composing with title in mind
to know limit
is not

journey of the linguit
is interface for translation
book as tactile memo trial
the turning of resisting

I am the audience unit
of my own company
set sun on stun

body, ultimate border
audience, ultimate enforcer
bleed the crossover

artist as junk space
the cognitive incompletist
the primal preset

contested space
how dare you call me protected
the omni present

if definition is the law
art is against the law
    john cage

what is possessed
by language will blur
    by language

crossing limit
by order this is not
    about crossing

but border when is
crossing
    transforming

when is border
    cause

bodies attempt
    walls scream

empirical tyranny
umbilical theory ... sure, sure ... listen,
more is the norm okay ...
more is normal, so
gimme a little less
some less to leave you with
the problem of thingness is presentation
material is thing, okay ... but so is next
right there, you left your n
before your ext—because I am limitless
I am shape-shifting demon
I am invocator
the apostrophic worker
taking pleasure in the frictive
space after speech

creature of pen reminds finger
will circulate always
through limbic speak—
I aestethically bore
the expert realster
did I say limitless … how g-force of me
to question everyone
by exclusion, what center
arrives complete … k(no)w not I
so why insist the limit
on the everyone-around-me, y'dig?

Ambient Language

Apparition of alphabet fire.Infant of Ambient Word.

idea is word in persona of skin

Ambient Typography

Mistranslation of the Ambient.

Ambient Collaboration

Ambient Learning

```
I'm-Being-Ent...
I'm Being Lent...
I'mmmm B'...
I'mmmma B'...
I'mmmma Being...Amma Viento
```

•

to a boy whose apparitions begin across the burning alphabet
father figure is set on fire by belonging

for counting by time —— space radars

Ambïent Typögraphy Collaboration

Misapplication of floor. Ambient. Infant of Ambient ord.

use your tongue all of em

I'm Being Eat : : : : · muy vientido

mmmma being

imaginary
wind-gates
where
head-mate
imagines

•

Breath is king-queen-country / *MoFaSiBro*
Breath is mother father sister brother
All in one / *MoFaSiBro*

Hysterial fusion.
Boschian tangents...if we could all breathe
As one

This all impossible
But I appear it on page, so
Becomes possible on way—through page

●

[BLOCKED TEARDUCT]

the largeness of the katydid ...

is that a spider is as big as a grasshopper
until its legs reach the size of your arms
stiffened juiceless by sunless static
the insect sleeping on your speakers
will crash your party stealing thunder
from your stage being your arms
when a gang of liquid griots scowl at your taking
of another bread slice your please in your quiver
setting off envy before task your man's role
squeezed out of your opening milk
is that the bird found walking will lend its feet
for a waxed image impressed on a moonwalker
to show how soft your man heart can be
when sailing through electronic fog
your insect arms the size of dolphins
will carry the tiny fisher who decides
on a decade while eating dust that whaling
to rattatatt the omniboys will sweep the surf
from your fingers being what pacifies your hide
when a riot of equillibrium slides the orange man
under blue mirror pulled over on slang making
small talk big before we've had a chance
to find out if rain will leave or if more will cry
when water from your eye can reach
the size of your pinky is when the ocean
will drown under the size of its reach

●

        [in one standing, one month
        will not make one year
        reach the end of your month and think you've done
        your month and realize the end of your month
is also the end of someone's month, your month shared with someone,
your finish shared outside your wish
        is dream . . . not standing, until you take
        timeline by its shake, in never-ending focus
        makes dream immobile, what gives pause its start
        taking one year for one finish will take someone else's
        for a shared ending, beginning
        what can only bend]

                            •

    Untactical
  . to mention hybrid species (i.e. dream)
    in talk of breath, yet ... very prognosis
    inherent of ambient age

    Gives me papers, y'dig ...
    to cross into foreign territory
    despite m'last name-ism
    —my road-obscured by anti-wallism

    A mere Latino, un-Latinized by non-Latino speak
    surrounded by sun and sound, the mark I leave—a field of words
    I'm trying to achieve nothing
    and leave no traces—lots of them

    Ambient Tangent
    transformation of ten thousand tangents
    into one Ambient Language—I'm-Beyond Tanguage
    —the eyesore of the hypnotist

•

been sitting in sun   watching m'mind move
trees say I'm berserk   no reason to doubt their flaws
these road sign are familiar   intimate in the sprawling landscape
with hand held out   I'm led to findings

gonna find two as the same   gonna find who has my name

wish I were standing on someone's shoulder
expanding my oral lips

my pants ride up   like a hero of mine I can't pronounce
lovely mosaic   cracked by split screams

what's inside this looking   but a zoo of arrangements

first hand out   my head   this skin
windowless sun on my windowhead
intimacy consumes

on a long walk in the sun I stay right here
crushing
the hypnotized grass

• • •

The PoPedology of an Ambient Language
was printed in an edition of 1000 copies
at Thomson-Shore, Inc.
Text design and typesetting by Edwin Torres
using Sabon for the text
and Compacta and Monaco
for subtitles and notations.
Cover art by Edwin Torres
"Mute Thunder" & "Ambient Language II" mixed media.

Edwin Torres was born in New York City. His books include *In The Function Of External Circumstances*, *The All-Union Day Of The Shock Worker*, and *Fractured Humorous*. His CDs include *Oceano Rise*, *Novo* and *Holy Kid*.

Atelos was founded in 1995 as a project of Hip's Road and is devoted to publishing, under the sign of poetry, writing that challenges conventional, limiting definitions of poetry.

All the works published as part of the Atelos project are commissioned specifically for it, and each is involved in some way with crossing traditional genre boundaries, including, for example, those that would separate theory from practice, poetry from prose, essay from drama, the visual image from the verbal, the literary from the non-literary, and so forth.

The Atelos project when complete will consist of 50 volumes.

The project directors and editors are Lyn Hejinian and Travis Ortiz. The director for text production and design is Travis Ortiz; the director for cover production and design is Ree Katrak.

Atelos (current volumes):

Distributed by:

Small Press Distribution
1341 Seventh Street
Berkeley, California
      94710-1403

Atelos
P O Box 5814
Berkeley, California
      94705-0814

to order from SPD call 510-524-1668 or toll-free 800-869-7553
fax orders to: 510-524-0852
order via e-mail at: orders@spdbooks.org
order online from: www.spdbooks.org